THE ROAD TO PURITY

THE ROAD TO PURITY

Setting Captives Free

T. CHARLES STEPHENS

To order additional copies of this book, contact:
Xlibris Corporation
1-888-795-4274
www.Xlibris.com
Orders@Xlibris.com
102787

CONTENTS

To my lovely wife, Paula, who is an angel on loan from God: All that I am, or hope to ever be, I owe to you.

To my son Tim: May God use your musical genius to change and inspire this generation.

To my daughter Maya: You have the keys that will unlock many scientific and curative mysteries. May God use you to bring health and healing to the nations.

Acknowledgments

Special thanks to Bishop George Dallas McKinney, whom God used to extricate me from the bonds of sin. Your compassion and service to the people of God are unsurpassed! May the Lord's grace and peace continually be upon you.

Eternal God our Father, when the heavens are shut and there is no rain because we have sinned against thee, we will confess thy name and turn from our sin. For thou hath said, "If my people, which are called by my name, shall humble themselves and pray, seek my face and turn from their wicked ways, then will I hear from heaven and will forgive their sin and will heal their land."

Preface

This book was born out of the darkest pages of my being. It is a culmination of events and experiences that led to my deliverance and total liberation from pornography.

Many books are available on the subject of how to be set free from the power of pornography. What I want to share doesn't come out of a book; it comes out of a life—a life filled with shame and condemnation, resulting in a total loss of dignity and pride.

Imagine yourself being freed from sexually explicit material. You have a bulletproof existence filled with the purity and virtue God intended for you to have—a life filled with his presence, filled with the joy and the splendor of God. Visualize yourself free from the addictive vices of sin. Envision the pleasure of knowing God out of a pure heart and mind.

Before my deliverance from porn, I heard countless stories of miraculous turnarounds of desperate circumstances. I was skeptical and sure that it wasn't true. I was equally sure it would never happen to me. But it did! And it can happen to you too!

You too can understand the fullness of joy as it relates to worshipping God, clean and free from the impurities of sin. When we live tainted lives as men of God, it's akin to bringing flowers home to our wives after just having sex with our girlfriends across town.

I'm writing this book to help others become free from the power that soils their lives—so they can become the bride the Lord is coming back to claim as his own. I hope this book will forever change your relationship with Christ, as well as change how you see yourself as a child of God. My prayer is that you will open your heart to receive his love so you can lay hold of his promises and everything his blood has purchased for you at Calvary's Cross.

Introduction

The struggle begins in the private part of our lives where fundamental decisions regarding morals, values, and ethics are formed. We are challenged the most in the area where our personal beliefs, primary faith, and convictions are determined. It is not because we doubt the ability of Christ, the One who alone has the power to redeem us. We are challenged because of our inability to trust him fully and have confidence in the redeeming power of his grace, which can make us entirely free.

In the Western civilization, there are inexhaustible possibilities for exploring every facet of immorality, which promises to fulfill our every desire. From cybersex to iPod sex, today's culture is simply overrun with options to help accomplish the basest forms of depraved living. During the seventies and eighties, buying pornography usually meant going to some seedy little store in a distasteful part of town. But the Internet (enter net) has taken away the embarrassment of facing those who peddle immorality. It has given us the ability to remain ambiguous as we secretly discover every aspect of moral corruption.

This is where the realm of secret kingdoms rule and govern our lives and is where the real danger lies. This is due in part because of the lack of accountability or genuine interaction with those who would hold us responsible.

This is also where the delusion of being able to handle our problems without help is birthed. Psalm 19:13 refers to this as presumptuous sins. These are sins we think we can handle on our own. At best, our lives remain broken, shattered, and unfulfilled because of the incessant belief that we are in control. In fact, the surreptitious immoral behavior we so affectionately adhere to is nothing more than a snare, appropriate to keep us from our God-given prominence as we seek his righteous cause on the earth.

Deficiency of the spirit is another culprit of our inability to govern our affairs on higher levels of holiness and spiritual success. Our failure to mature spiritually is the root cause of the individuals who appear to be religious, when in fact the very foundations of their lives are ready to collapse. This is due in part to a failure to dominate the salacious materials that subjugate our lives daily. This relates to man's failure to connect on higher levels with the Spirit of the living God, which in turn, causes us to settle for the outward show of looking victorious, while our private lives are in utter disarray. This mind-set lends credence to the scripture, which states that men would have a form of godliness, denying the true power thereof. Simply put, we would rather *look* the part than *become* the part.

As we reflect on the foregone conclusions, let us presume that if we are to influence this generation for Christ and become men and women others can benefit from, then we must lay aside everything that obscures the voice of God from our hearts. We must renounce the hidden things that prohibit stability and bring order to the private regions of our lives by repudiating the crippling effects of sin.

In this book, we will uncover some of the root causes that lead to the nauseous behavior we utterly detest. We will also learn how to break the generational curses handed down by our fathers.

You no longer have to be mastered by the waywardness of your circumstances. You too can be set free! It's time to let your *amen* become a reality!

Chapter 1

Every Man's Fight

Fight the good fight of the faith; lay hold of the eternal life to which you were summoned and [for which] you confessed the good confession [of faith] before many witnesses.

—1 Timothy 6:12 (AMP)

We are to fight the good fight of faith, which means we must fight to do what is right, simply because it's right. It's called the good fight of faith, because faith always wins.

The first step in fighting the good fight is to get connected with the body of Christ. You cannot be detached from the church and expect to win, because the fight is not yours to battle alone. It's a shared fight where we employ our gifts and join our faith with other believers.

If you call yourself a Christian but do not go to church regularly or will not connect with others of like faith on deeper levels, you will eventually embody the position of a formalist—someone who seems religious and places strong or excessive emphasis on the outward appearance, instead of possessing a meaningful inner life. Others may actually see some resemblance of Christ in a formalist from time to time but without any real evidence of true conformity to his will.

The church is filled with formalists and religious people who would rather straddle the fence of indecision regarding their convictions than take a stand and remain firm on what they know to be the truth of God's Word. Those who fall into this category will find it difficult to ascertain the deeper things of God or come to the level of spiritual authority that is promised to every believer, simply because it requires a level of self-sacrifice and denial beyond what most people are willing to allow.

Many people in the body of Christ do not mind experiencing the power of his resurrection. It is the fellowship of his suffering they contend with. I call it the Peter Principle. This is the aspect of our relationship with the Lord where we are content to follow him in the face of adversity, just from a great distance. We really don't mind following him as long as it does not become an offense to others or a detriment to ourselves.

The Lord knew Peter would fall. He also knew Peter would get back up. Peter's failure didn't catch God off guard, and your failures don't either. But when you systematically determine to override the Word of God to embrace the prior arrangements of sin, you have nothing more than a relationship of convenience, which always provides an exit strategy when it becomes necessary.

The fight for purity is every man's fight and must be won at all costs. The message of purity must be unmistakably pronounced to the world, but the cleansing must begin at the house of God.

It is a sad commentary, but some of the large hotel chains have stated that they love it when Christians hold conferences at their hotels, because that's when they make the most money from pornography. According to an article written in the *Christian Science Monitor*, surveys showed that 40 million Americans regularly view Internet pornography, which accounts for $2.5 billion of the $12 billion US porn industry. Some 25 percent of search engine requests were porn related; 20 percent of men and 13 percent of women admitted accessing porn at work. A survey published in a *Leadership Journal* stated that 37 percent of the pastors said that pornography was a struggle for them, and 51 percent admitted it was a temptation.

How can we as believers expect to present the pureness, wholesomeness, strength, vibrancy, richness, and depth of Christ's love to a dying world when we ourselves are impure? We live in a day of excess—a day where seemingly anything imaginable can be achieved through the stroke of a key on a computer. It is a hypersexual culture, which has the ability to arouse and stimulate us but cannot fill the empty spaces of our hearts, cannot give us rest, and cannot gratify the vacant places of our lives. We live in a porn-centric society where we depend on our sensory acuities to appease the desires of our flesh; unfortunately, we are not rational enough to understand that the stimuli we choose are incapable of bringing us long-term fulfillment.

What your spirit yearns for is Christ; what your spirit craves for is worship. Due to our fallen natures, we try to fill the void in our hearts with natural appetites and carnalities of the flesh, and so we make worse our dilemma by not realizing that we can never make content the flesh. You cannot satisfy your spirit through carnal activities of the flesh. The flesh will take you where you don't want to go, keep you longer than you want to stay, and make you do things you said you'd never do. So wicked is the flesh that we cannot negotiate or confer with it, and so we should avoid flirting with it at all cost.

The Bible says the only way to adequately deal with our fallen nature is to mortify its deeds.

> For if you live according to [the dictates of] the flesh, you will
> surely die. But if through the power of the [Holy] Spirit you
> are [habitually] putting to death (making extinct, deadening)
> the [evil] deeds prompted by the body, you shall [really and
> genuinely] live forever.[2]

And so we secure our lives by following the Spirit, tending to those things that bring us into a closer relationship with the true and living God.

However, we cannot put an end to our carnal desires in and of our own strength. Putting an end to the deeds of the flesh is accomplished by the aid of the Holy Spirit, helping our spirit in the effort. For as many as who are led by the Spirit of God, they are the sons of God. This means that those who "mortify the deeds of the flesh through the Spirit" are led by the Spirit. They obey the spirit rather than the flesh. The presence of the Spirit in leading them shows they are God's sons. The real question is, do you want to be led by the Spirit? Do you want your Christianity to work? Then you must seek Jesus for the answers to the problems you face, realizing it is not by your capacity or by your power that you overcome; it's by his Spirit.

Some of the struggles we face regarding purity are inherent to our childhood, while others relate to learned behavior and certain underlying issues. The challenge to be free of pornography is a daily fight. Many are losing the battle primarily because they are not skilled enough to combat the forces that come against them or simply don't understand the logistics of living in a society that has chosen to live without Christ!

Prophet Daniel lived in a similar culture but kept his integrity. He understood how to live holy in an unholy world. Twenty-first-century charismatic believers, though, have lost sight of the principles of living morally and spiritually perfect in a world where we are inundated on every front with sexually suggestive material. From television to radio and from books to magazines, society, at large, is preoccupied with stimuli that affect every sensory area of our lives.

Furthermore, there is no denying that the adversary has infiltrated particular aspects of our lives without consent. To eradicate this problem, we must face it head-on. Otherwise we will remain shackled to the beggarly elements of life and continue to exist in a state of spiritual and moral decline.

One of the first steps in breaking the chains that hold us captive is to admit that we have difficulty with the unrelenting appetites of our flesh. We must come to terms with the fact that we function as weak strong men in the kingdom and that the secrecy by which we licentiously operate is nothing more than a cloak for the enemy to work behind, which ultimately keeps us from growing in our faith.

The only real solution to the problem of impurity is to open our hearts completely to God's love, realizing that he cares for you and has a plan of restoration for your life. Opening your heart to his infinite love is the only way to position yourself to receive the healing you've needed for so long. You no longer have to live a life of spiritual obscurity and shame or wear the grave clothes of sin. His grace is sufficient for you, and his mercy endures forever. When the adversary points to your indiscretions and demands payment for your sins, the blood of Jesus will always speak on your behalf, reminding the enemy that the price has already been paid. Grace and mercy are kinsmen who will stand and speak on your behalf as well. Grace, which is the unmerited favor of God, allows you to receive that which you do not deserve, while mercy keeps you from getting what you do deserve!

Your role is simply to repent and turn from sin. You need to know you can live free from the power of darkness so that you can take your rightful place in the Kingdom of God and fulfill all God has purposed for your life. Categorically, you must come to the place where your love for God supersedes all else, including your fear of what others may think or say, especially as it relates to your healing.

I have witnessed many men in church shrink at the point of opportunity when breakthrough seemed imminent, only to leave the service the same way they came in—broken and without hope. Why? They were simply unable to run to Jesus with an uncontrollable disregard for the inconsequential opinion of others. They failed to realize that the ground at the foot of the Cross is the most level place where sinners stand to be set free. In the house of God, there is no condemnation. There is not one person in the church who doesn't have problems. The devil is the one who makes us feel condemned by suggesting thoughts such as follows: How can you be saved and be the way you are? He then translates those feelings into ideas that God is the one pointing the finger of condemnation at us. God does not point his finger. He reaches out to you with his nail-scarred hand!

You must get to a point in your life where it doesn't matter who knows your particular situation or who is in attendance when the call for prayer is given. Naturally speaking, when you have fallen into a deep pit and have been there for a while with no hope of getting out on your own, you don't care who is standing on the other end of the rope as you're pulled to safety. You just want out!

You must approach your deliverance from pornography with the same incentive and stop denying the tug on your heart when those who minister give the appeal that fits your circumstances. Complacency and apathy will water down your breakthrough like a drunken stupor. There is a rich harvest with your name on it. Lives hang in the balance; souls teeter on the brink of destruction waiting on the manifestations of the sons of God—waiting on you to influence your generation for the glory of God.

But these are lives you will not impact until you get free of the things that subdue you and cause recidivism in your life. You must come to the realization that the propitious smiles of heaven cannot be realized until your purity becomes a reality! In the final analysis, what you are dealing with is not even about you; it's about you overcoming the spiritual ineptitudes of life so you can impact the lives of those you are called to inspire. Understanding the call on your life is very important, because it is where your restoration is set in motion. Determining that you are part of a universal plan to bring men into unification with God is where the mind-set to be free is born.

Even if you are currently in the mire of sin, call upon the Lord to help you. Humble yourself under the mighty hand of God, for he will not forsake you. The Holy Spirit has been instructed to resist the proud but give grace to the humble. Humility and eagerness to please God is where the Lord stands and listens for the cries of those who have fallen and say, "Help me, Holy Spirit!"

This is also the place where he gathers the tears of our contrition and helps the inarticulate stammering sounds of those who have stumbled but have humbled themselves to pray.

When you are afflicted and so far down that you have to look up to see the bottom, call on the Holy Spirit. He will then shift from his role of comforting you to untangling you from whatever difficulties you face. He literally gets into the pit where you are tied, gagged, and bound to set you free. Unequivocally, the Holy Spirit hates every one of your infirmities and will fight against the things that have come to destroy your life. He will, with your permission, get into whatever situation you face to set you at liberty so you can accomplish the mandate God has upon your life.

Chapter 2

Thirty-Three Years of Bondage

I am the Lord, and I will bring you out from under the burdens of the Egyptians, and I will free you from their bondage, and I will rescue you with an outstretched arm [with special and vigorous action] and by mighty acts of judgment.

—Exodus 6:6 (AMP)

There was a Jewish festival for which Jesus went up to Jerusalem. Now there is in Jerusalem a pool near the Sheep Gate. This pool in the Hebrew is called Bethesda, having five porches. In these lay a great number of sick folk—some blind, some crippled, and some paralyzed (shriveled up)—waiting for the bubbling up of the water. For an angel of the Lord went down at appointed seasons into the pool and moved and stirred up the water; whoever then first, after the stirring up of the water, stepped in was cured of whatever disease with which he was afflicted. There was a certain man there who had suffered with a deep-seated and lingering disorder for thirty-eight years. When Jesus noticed him lying there [helpless], knowing that he had already been a long time in that condition, He said to him, do you want to become well? [Are you really in earnest about getting well?] The invalid answered, Sir, I have nobody when the water is moving to put me into the pool; but while I am trying to come [into it] myself, somebody else steps down ahead of me. Jesus said to him,

Get up! Pick up your bed and walk! Instantly the man became well
and recovered his strength and picked up his bed and walked.

—John 5:1-9 (AMP)

The pool at Bethesda represents the condition of countless lives in the church today. It symbolizes the disorder of those who have been in the same position for many years—the position of doubt, indifference, and refusal. Blind, halt, and maimed, they long for someone to help them, but no one seems to have the answers to their dilemmas. I believe many good men and women want to be set free from addictions but somehow can no longer visualize themselves not being bound or unrestrained. It may even appear to them that everyone else is going free except for them.

The five porches in this passage represent five levels, which include sickness and disease, poverty and lack, fear and torment, religion and tradition, and finally the flesh, which says it's all about me. Bethesda means "house of mercy," which ironically should point to Calvary where our healing was secured.

I believe there are two specific reasons that keep people from getting healed. Notice the verse that says, "In these *lay* a great multitude of impotent folk, of blind, *halt*, and withered." The word *lay* denotes refusal to get up or total acceptance of one's condition. The word *halt* shows someone who wavers and is unconvinced of the power that can set them totally free. When you refuse to change your ways or when your faith has diminished to the point where you begin to doubt the truth of God's Word, then your healing will no doubt be on hold. It is not because it's the will of God, who actually wants you to be free, but because of your inability to trust his Word.

When Jesus saw this man, the first thing he asked him was thus: Wilt thou be made whole? The question seems unnecessary; of course, the man wanted to be made whole. Jesus knew this but simply wanted to revive this man's faith by having him express his desire to be free. Sometimes when sickness, disease, or addictions become chronic, people tend to accept their condition as normal. But the articulation of one's desire to change begins the process of activating faith for their restoration.

The curious thing in this passage is that the man didn't know to whom he was speaking. Like many today, he was looking for a man, but he didn't recognize the man. We simply don't spot the Lord when he comes to church. We are so bound by tradition that we think we have to wait until the end of the service to get healed. I am so ready to see someone desperate enough to crawl to the altar while the announcements are being read and cry out to God to make them whole!

This man no longer had to wait for the moving of the water; the one who commanded the angel to go down was there in person. He was actually talking to the one who alone had the power to resuscitate his mortal body. Many times people go to the house of God expecting help from others, when Christ is standing there ready to do the work himself. Sadly, like the man in this story, many go to church for years but never get healed of their infirmities.

Jesus said something the man never expected. He said, "Rise, take up thy bed and walk." In other words, "Change your position of thinking, your position of sowing, and your position of speaking." If God be for you, then stir up the favor of God by activating your faith. When someone asks you how you are feeling, don't confess that you've never felt worse. Tell them you feel good by faith. Stop putting negative words into the atmosphere for the enemy to use against you. The power of life and death is in the tongue!

Finally, Jesus found the man in the temple later and said, "Behold, thou art made whole. Sin no more lest a worse thing come unto thee."

When you get set free, the absolute worst thing you can do is renegotiate with sin; this will always leave you in a much poorer state than before. You need to know there are worse levels than the previous five mentioned here.

My bondage goes back to my childhood where my most basic memories are dysfunctional at best. My father, who failed to perform the basic functions as the patriarch of our family, left the home when I was less than a year old, creating an empty place in my heart that took years to fill. My mother, who was left with the daunting task of raising three small children on her own, decided she too needed to be unrestrained and left a year and a half later.

I was almost three years old when she walked out of our lives. I remember that cold rainy night like it was yesterday. The childlike uncertainty of what was taking place still lingers in my mind. I remember being awakened that night by my mom, who exclaimed that we needed to hurry and get dressed because the cab was almost there! I didn't quite know what was going on but hurried along with my brother and sister to get dressed. The cab arrived, and we were whisked off to a hotel, where we stayed for about an hour or so before going over to our grandparents' house.

When we finally arrived at our grandparents', it was evident something was very wrong. My brother and sister began to cry as my mom headed for the front door. I ran to her, clinging to her side as I often did, and asked, "Where are you going, Mommy?"

She replied, "Just down the street. Don't worry. I'll be right back."

I waited and waited for my mom to return that night, but she never came back.

The next time I saw her was eight years later at the funeral of my grandmother, who had passed away just days before. My feelings about seeing my mom again were ambivalent and filled with pain. I despised my mom for leaving me, especially with my grandmother whose ominous demeanor was unrivaled. My grandmother often physically and verbally abused my brother and me, causing us to feel frightened and very alone.

Little did I know that the adversary, through the spirit of fear, would stop me from achieving the success God wanted me to have for years to come. The aches and pains of not feeling wanted and loved by my mom and dad was the bedrock of my addiction. These feelings led to many secret kingdoms, which allowed me to rule but oddly held me captive for a very long time, causing my life to spiral completely out of control.

I entered the adult world of pornography at the age of twelve when I stumbled upon some obscene magazines, which belonged to some friends of my mom who moved in with us for a while. My hunger for pornography developed from a childlike curiosity, which led to an addiction that took over thirty years to break. While it seemed innocent at first, my appetite for porn became more and more incessant. At first, my eagerness to explore this new world was somewhat childish. I would rush home from school and go straight to my bedroom, where I would explore and delve deeper into this newfound interest. It didn't take long, however, for my desire for sexual material to increase. As a matter of fact, throughout adolescence and well into adulthood, the pornography that I used became more extreme. It has to in order to keep the viewer's interest. From print to video, from the Internet to real-life encounters, upgrading became absolutely necessary. By the age of eighteen, the beast had taken over.

This very detestable habit formed out of a secrecy that developed into a way of life that led me down many dark paths. From the age of twelve to the age of forty-three, I was bound by an addiction that demanded that I feed it more and more each passing day. I had become enslaved by the unfortunate tendencies of my past.

The stage was set, and the die was cast for my life to plummet downward through a lifestyle of self-indulgent behavior.

This left me the victim of a more sinister obstacle called self-denial. There was a time when I could not talk about my addiction due in part to self-denial. The covert nature of denial always lurks behind the shadows of prideful thinking and one's inability to admit that something very immoral does exist. I believe that any level of success as it relates to a deliverance from pornography is directly proportionate to one's ability to eliminate pride and the self-serving attitude that suggests there isn't really a problem—or, worse, you can handle the problem by yourself. Humility allows us to receive the help God sends to us through the lives of others who have overcome, as well as those whom he has chosen to walk with us through our struggles in life.

My personal deliverance from pornography began when I told my wife the truth about what I had hidden from her for so many years. It took a great deal of humbleness to get to the point where I could admit to her I needed help. I was mortified at the thought of telling her about my secret life. But I knew it was imperative to do so because I hadn't just hurt myself; I had hurt her too! The healing I needed would begin with confessing my faults to her and asking for forgiveness. She had been victimized for years by double standards and by the duplicitous way in which I lived. I did not belong to her wholeheartedly, and a lot of what she experienced in our marriage was due to my inability to love her without a divided heart. I loved her, but I also loved the secret domain where I was the head of state.

What do you do when you are in the middle of two things that vie for your utmost affection? In retrospect, you terminate everything that dishonors God. You must come to terms with the fact that some things will compete for your purity and the sanctity of your marriage for the rest of your life. The question is, will you choose to do that which honors God or give in to the inappropriate behavior of your flesh? I chose the road of honor, which meant that I would repair the breach of my marriage by admitting I had not kept the covenant that was established between my wife and me almost sixteen years earlier. I was embarrassed to face her because of the high esteem in which she held me as a man of God.

I had accepted my call into the ministry just after our first year of marriage, but most of the time, I felt hypocritical and worthless because of my inclinations toward pornography. My hypocrisy as a minister drove me deeper into myself and away from those who loved me the most. I began to sense a paradigm shift. I wasn't sure, but for the first time in the sixteen years of our marriage I wanted to tell my wife about my addiction. God was dealing with me about confessing my faults to her. I thought, *No way—I can't do it!*

So I began to rebuke what God was trying to do through confession. I thought, *Why bring it up? What she doesn't know won't hurt her.* That's a lie, and if you buy into it, you will not get healed! Spare the gory details if you will; she doesn't have to know all the particulars of your objectionable deeds. But if you're going to come from behind the shadows of your past, you must clear your conscience and reinstate your relationship with her through the pathway of purity, but confession must lead the way. Otherwise the pretense will continue. I was the priest of the home, but in reality, I had adopted a pharisaical spirit that caused me to look spiritual without real power.

I will never forget the evening I called my wife into the bedroom so we could talk. I started out by telling her I was not the man she thought I was and that I had lived a lie all the previous years of our marriage. I told her face-to-face that I was hooked on Internet pornography. I stood there for a moment, bracing myself for the fallout of what I had just confessed.

Instead, my wife, with the face of an angel, looked at me with a calmness that could only come from God and uttered these words: "Get up, man of God! Get up!"

The courage, faith, and unconditional love she displayed for me that evening was the start of my healing process. I felt peace and sudden joy brought on by not having to hide or carry this thing any longer. For the first time since my addiction I felt the six-hundred-pound gorilla on my back called lust loosen his hold. I wasn't fully delivered, but I felt a shift.

We soon moved to San Diego, where my wife had accepted a position with a national television affiliate. We had begun to look for a church home, when we happened upon a local church in the community where we lived. I now know it was a divine appointment.

The pastor concluded the service that morning with an altar call for men who were struggling with pornography. He stated that there was grace for us. He further stated that he wanted to pray for our deliverance. I thought, *He's got to be kidding if he thinks I'm going to expose myself in front of all these strangers. Doesn't he understand that this is private? After all, I don't need any help. I can handle it on my own.* Reality, however, is more authentic than fantasy, and opportunity is concerned with only the future and not the past. The fact is, if I could have handled it on my own, I would have.

As I thought about going up for prayer, I became filled with apprehension; fear immobilized me. As I sat there, I began to deny what God was doing in and through this pastor. When suddenly it happened, I stood up and began to walk toward the altar. The room grew still as I made my way to the front of the church. Stumbling through tears and years of heartache and pain, I made my way to Jesus as he embraced and welcomed me into fellowship with the Father.

At first, everything seemed surreal, but with every step I took, I sensed a deeper realization of what was taking place. I felt a great determination to be free from the chains that held me captive for over thirty years. For the first time in my life, I had become transparent in the midst of others. I no longer cared who was watching. I felt the overwhelming power of the Holy Spirit illuminate my heart and release me from the dungeon of pornography. God wasn't mad at me as I had thought; instead, I felt the magnificent power of his love cleanse me from my sins. He healed my soul through the wonders of his grace, mercy, and tenderness.

Immediately and without delay, I knew it was over. I knew in an instant that God had done a complete work in my heart. Instantaneously God had removed what had taken me over thirty years to build. I give God the praise!

I can't remember how life used to be when I was a prisoner to the sin that had me bound for so long. Yes, I still get tempted, and, yes, it's a daily fight to remain pure. In fact, I must live an absolute lifestyle of discipline. The fact that I have been delivered does not mean I can let my guard down. I cannot control what the enemy throws at me. But I can control how I react to every situation. Life is 10 percent of what happens to you; the other 90 percent is how you respond. Temptation will always show up at my doorway. It will always knock, but when it does, I simply look at Jesus and ask him to get the door for me.

Chapter 3

Why You Must Win This Battle

For [even the whole] creation (all nature) waits expectantly and longs earnestly for God's sons to be made known [waits for the revealing, the disclosing of their sonship].

—Romans 8:19 (AMP)

The return of Christ is not a theory for you to debate or a fable for you to ignore. It is not a riddle for you to solve. It is, in fact, one of the most important truths of our age, not merely to understand or agree with but to anticipate, embrace, and live out.

I believe this not only because of my unshakable confidence in what the Bible says about the future, but also because of recent world events that draw me to the conclusion that he is coming very soon. I want you to understand that these events fit into God's prophetic timetable for the world, Israel, and you. I want you to grasp the outcome. I want this to be a wake-up call for you so you will understand that the prophesied events are fast approaching and will affect you. There is no neutral ground; you're either for him or against him. You need to know that, no matter what, God is in complete control, and his will is going to be accomplished.

This is not the time to be lukewarm or to procrastinate. There is no time for complacency or mental assent, which is where many people have gone through the head steps of getting set free from pornography but never really take the required action to set the decision in motion. Purity is a fight that you must win if you are going to be used by God to your fullest!

One of the greatest tragedies in life is to watch people waste the potential God has placed within them. Modern life and contemporary events create a deceptive appearance that is meant to please or impress others but is really false and superficial. It displays the veneer of success without real progress or personal development in the private area of our lives. True success, both private and public, comes from finding God's purpose for your life and fulfilling it. Winning the battle for purity and maintaining sobriety starts with putting a stop to the soulless manipulation of sin by adapting ourselves to the reality that there is a private domain that exists within us.

In addition, bringing order to that realm is essential if we are to receive the awaiting benefits God has for everyone who will be conformed to his image. The primary purpose of order is to develop spiritual growth and personal progress through the utilization of spiritual skill sets that include, but are not limited to, prayer, fasting, spending time in the Word, use of time, applied wisdom, and accountability. In order to live our lives according to his will and reach the lost, we must discover these truths and learn to apply them, which will help us equip and empower others with whom we live, work, and worship.

Refusal to recognize these facts usually results in years of wasted potential and missed opportunities. One of the ironies of living this way as a Christian is that it lends to powerless living, apathy, lethargy, and mediocrity. Our influence and impact on the lives of others is put on hold while we remain content to pacify our lust. There are people waiting on you to speak and make a difference in their lives! You might be thinking that you couldn't possibly make a difference in the lives of others.

Maybe you've heard the story of a young man on the beach throwing starfish into the sea, based on the story by Loren Eisley. It states thus: "I awoke early, as I often did, just before sunrise to walk by the ocean's edge and greet the new day. As I moved through the misty dawn, I focused on a faint, faraway motion. I saw a youth, bending and reaching and flailing his arms, dancing on the beach, no doubt in celebration of the perfect day soon to begin.

"As I approached, I sadly realized the youth was not dancing to the bay but rather bending to sift through the debris left by the night's tide, stopping to pick up a starfish and then standing, to heave it back into the sea. I asked the youth the purpose of the effort.

"'The tide has washed the starfish onto the beach, and they cannot return to the sea by themselves,' the youth replied. 'When the sun rises, they will die, unless I throw them back to the sea.'

"As the youth explained, I surveyed the vast expanse of beach, stretching in both directions beyond my sight. Starfish littered the shore in numbers beyond calculation. The hopelessness of the youth's plan became clear to me, and I countered, 'But there are more starfish on this beach than you can ever save before the sun is up. Surely you cannot expect to make a difference.'

"The youth paused briefly to consider my words, bent to pick up a starfish, and threw it as far as possible. Turning to me, he simply said, 'I made a difference to that one.' I left the boy and went home, deep in thought of what the boy had said. I returned to the beach and spent the rest of the day helping the boy throw starfish into the sea."

You can make the difference too! One way to begin is by taking authority over the secretive areas of your life, which will ultimately bring stability to those private places. Carnality prohibits you from impacting others. You must move beyond self-imposed limitations brought on by certain inconsistencies that relate to your growth as a son of God. No longer can you afford to look as if you are Spirit-filled; you must become Spirit-filled, which will prove to be a positive force in the lives of those you interact with on a daily basis.

It is said we create the behavior we fear the most. You can no longer afford to negotiate compromise with your own values. If you find yourself repeating bad deeds, you must look at the root cause of the problem. When I see the lack of spiritual growth in Christian men, my only question is, what sins have they not dealt with? What keeps them from coming into his glory, into his presence? Whatever you are, you must win over the things that cause you to return to the desert places of life. Otherwise you will not have the spiritual authority to speak into the lives of your sons and daughters. You cannot have authority over that which you have not overcome!

One of the biggest mistakes I made when my son was entering adolescence was to tell him not to get involved with pornography while I was still using it myself. Although what I was telling him was right, I had no authority to countermand the attacks that he would face. Telling him not to do something that I was still engaged in opened a legal entry point for certain demonic persuasions to come into his life. The spiritual principle I misunderstood was that our children would fight the same battles we as fathers fail to win, whether it's with anger issues, addictive destructive behavior, or extramarital affairs. What you don't win over your sons will live to fight, and their sons, because you cannot free your children if you are not free yourself. In essence, you must identify that which you must confront and confront that which you must conquer.

The enemy, in his relentless pursuit to overtake you, checks every door to your heart daily to see which one you've left unlocked. If you leave the door to lust and perversion unlocked, that's the door the enemy will use to get a foothold in your life.

At some point, someone has to say enough is enough! You must apply the blood over the doorpost of your heart, sealing off every access. After all, you're not fighting for your future alone; you're fighting for the virtue and integrity of your sons, as well as the innocence of your daughters. You set the stage for their victories in life, as well as their downfalls.

During World War II, there was a man by the name of Butch O'Hare. O'Hare Field in Chicago is named after him. He was one of the aviation heroes of World War II. Butch O'Hare, while stationed in the Pacific Ocean, went out on a mission in his fighter plane one day and realized they hadn't topped off his fuel tank. He told his squad leader, who told him to return to the ship because he would run out of gas before the mission was complete.

As Butch was flying back to the fleet, he noticed a whole squadron of Japanese planes, bombers, and zeros. He was the only protection in the air to keep the fleet of the US naval ships from being seriously damaged. He took no thought for his life and began to attack the squadron of enemy planes. Butch O'Hare shot down six different enemy planes and when he ran out of ammunition tried to clip off their wings. He darted in and through until the whole Japanese formation became disassembled and headed back to their home base without dropping a bomb, or firing a torpedo at the US fleet.

With his plane seriously shot up, Butch managed to land on the carrier. He later received many awards, including the Congressional Medal of Honor given to him by President Roosevelt. The president stated that in all probability, Butch O'Hare was the most heroic individual who had ever fought and flown a plane for the United States. A year later, Butch went back into combat and was killed in action.

I think it's safe to say Butch O'Hare was built with the right stuff. Someone in his life had taught him the right principles.

Let's look at a contrasting figure. During the Roaring Twenties, there was a man by the name of Al Capone who was one of the most famous and powerful gangsters in the US history. During the 1920s, he built a criminal empire in Chicago that became the model for the present-day organized crime.

He had an attorney named Easy Eddie. Eddie was a brilliant man who kept Capone out of jail for many years. He and Capone were in business together and became very rich. Easy Eddie was the legal arm of Al Capone's machinery of criminology, including paybacks, kickbacks, and all kinds of other illegal operations. Eddie lived a jeweled life. Capone once gave him a whole block to live on complete with maids, servants, and limousines.

Easy Eddie had all the money in the world, but he lived a double life. He lived the life of a criminal, and then he lived a life with his family, particularly with his son, whom he took to church every Sunday, teaching him right from wrong. Eddie was interested in his son becoming the right kind of person in the world.

Somewhere along the way, Easy Eddie became convicted of his life of crime and knew somehow he had to get his name straightened out because one day he would leave that name to his son. And so he contacted the federal authorities and turned the state's evidence, exposing Al Capone and testifying against him in a court of law. He knew that when he did that, Capone would put out a contract on him. He knew he was risking his life to tell the truth and cleanse his name for his son. Sure enough, one year later, almost to the day on which he testified against Capone, he was gunned down on a street in Chicago. Easy Eddie knew a great name was more desired than great riches. He further knew that unless he changed his ways, his son would live to fight the same battles he did. You see, Easy Eddie was Butch O'Hare's father.

Don't think for one minute that you can perpetrate deception and expect your children not to be affected, because children don't do as we say; they do as we do. The harvest God has for you include the success of future generations. Make a choice to change your ways; don't continue in sin; stop crucifying the Lord afresh; discontinue frustrating his grace.

If you can trust him to save you, why not trust him to deliver and keep you. Ask God to break up the deep places in your heart and release the fountains of your life. Martin Luther said that tears are heart water that until the fountains of the great deep of our lives are broken up, the heavens can't open up. We live in a world where we have a lot of stuff pinned up inside us that we've never wept over. There's a harvest you can't even get to until you learn how to cry.

Chapter 4

Warfare

This charge and admonition I commit in trust to you, Timothy, my son, in accordance with prophetic intimations which I formerly received concerning you, so that inspired and aided by them you may wage the good warfare.

—1 Timothy 1:18 (AMP)

I don't know what spiritual warfare means to you, but to me, it's not just taking authority over the works of darkness. It's about discovering the sovereignty of God, his majesty, and the supremacy of Christ. It's about discovering a peace in Christ so concrete that your faith becomes impervious to the attacks of the enemy! Being persistent is the key between winning and losing the war on purity. Persistence breaks resistance! The opposition of demons and their refusal to give in can be broken through the power of persistence. If you can persevere, if you can prevail, you can and will be victorious.

Learn to exercise dominion and take authority over every situation in your life. Learn to live so that faith becomes a daily appetite. Tell the devil he's no longer going to hold you hostage to your past. Keep in mind that engaging in warfare does not always mean you are going to be delivered out of the problem. Sometimes being set free means you'll be developed while going through the problem. You just need to make up your mind to serve God by not standing on the sidelines.

There's no neutral ground in the process of maintaining your freedom from sin. You must fight. There are no in-between positions or straddling the fence. You have undoubtedly seen men standing on fences, leaning on fences, or hanging on fences. But it is doubtful you will ever see a man straddling a fence. Any man would attest to the fact that fence straddling is not good for one's health. Nor is it good for your spiritual well-being. You simply cannot afford to straddle the fence of indecision regarding whose side you are fighting on. Doing so will certainly result in a treasonous ending. You're either for God or against him. Choose this day whom you will serve!

The combat for which we are to prepare for is not against ordinary human enemies. Although there may be times when it seems as if your closest loved one is acting like the devil, the old cliché about knocking the devil out of him or her is simply that—a cliché. You will not win what is meant to be fought in the spirit through the arm of emotionalism or physical confrontation. The only way you can defeat a situation orchestrated by Satan is by fighting it on your knees, for we wrestle not against flesh and blood. You are dealing with an enemy who is subtle—an enemy who uses wiles and stratagems to overtake us. He has a thousand and one ways of beguiling our minds and charming our hearts. Hence he is called a serpent for subtlety, an old serpent, experienced in the art and trade of tempting even the strongest of men. He is a powerful enemy in charge of principalities, powers, and rulers. They are numerous, they are vigorous, and they are spiritual in nature, which complicates matters because they are unseen.

The sooner you realize we are in a state of war, the sooner you'll prepare yourself for the battle. We get into trouble when we cease to be on the alert. The adversary knows the battlefield of spiritual warfare starts in your mind. He knows that if he can conquer some territory in your thoughts, he can set up a strategic position and from that place harass you all the time. He will try every day to take more and more territory until he gets you away from your walk with the Lord. He preys on the weak, the naive, and the unsuspecting. Weakness is a tent the devil pitches in your mind, your will, and your emotions so he can get a deeper foothold into your private affairs.

Lack of self-control, which is an incompatible position for the believer, is part of the problem. Self-indulgence is a territory that has been conquered and acquired by the enemy that needs to be arrested.

Let's get one thing straight. There's a devil loose, and you are in a fight! So stop trying to take a neutral stand or have mixed emotions about whose side you are fighting on. When it comes down to it, you have to hate sin to the point that you're willing to eradicate it at any cost.

You can no longer afford to give into the sundry emotionalisms of your heart regarding warfare—in which your mind declares war on sin, but your heart is missing in action. In the end, not only will you suffer defeat, your family will lose as well. The spirit behind the thing you are fighting is not satisfied with just ruining your life; it wants to destroy the purpose for which you were put on the earth for generations to come. Your spouse is not the problem. The problem is that you don't recognize the spirit orchestrating the attack through the loved ones with whom you interact. Instead of taking aim on the one who is the real perpetrator, you strike out against whoever is available, usually your wife and kids. Through covert attacks and systematic strikes by the enemy, you get hit repeatedly without any regard or spiritual retaliation on your part whatsoever.

It's bad enough to be in a fight, but it's much worse to be in a fight and not get in a lick. When my son was three years old, he would get into daily skirmishes with another little boy at his preschool. As soon as these boys were within two feet of each other, it was game on. My wife was very upset at the thought of our son fighting and could not bear the notion of his getting hurt.

One day after school, he came home with a note from his teacher stating that he had been fighting again with the other little boy that day. My wife demanded that I do something. I looked at her and said, "Yes, dear. You're right. I'll handle it." As she left the room, I turned to my son and quietly asked, "Did you get a lick in?" Of course, I was not serious. I didn't want my son or anyone else to get hurt.

Metaphorically speaking, when fighting the adversary, you can no longer afford not to get in a lick. What does that mean? It means, the next time you have the opportunity to watch something lewd on television, you simply turn it off. It means giving the devil a black eye by choosing the road of righteousness. Otherwise you're going to get hit again and again until you learn how to fight. If you are watching lewd movies on television or on the Internet, then don't expect the devil to leave you alone!

Do you remember the movie *Back to the Future*? In this movie, there was a character named George who portrayed a weakling, who was afraid to stand up to one of his aggressors named Biff. There was a scene in the movie, where Biff was twisting the arm of George, who by the way was standing up for a young lady that Biff was trying to take advantage of. This was the most pivotal moment in the movie. If George succumbs to fear and turns his back on the situation, he would lose the possibility of this girl becoming his future wife. What did George do as he stood crouched over in pain while Biff twisted his arm? He got in a lick! He stood up to the one who appeared to have the upper hand and planted one right on the nose of the bully. Edmund Burke said that the only thing necessary for evil to triumph is for good men to stand by and do nothing. Biff apparently had a glass jaw and got knocked out.

The devil has a glass jaw too. He just wants you to think he's incapable of being beat. He's already been defeated; you just need to walk in the victory that Jesus secured for you at the Cross. The Bible says we should be sober and vigilant because our adversary the devil, as a roaring lion, walks about, seeking whom he may devour. The devil was defanged at Calvary, but he is still a worthy adversary. Remember that he comes to steal, kill, and destroy. It's what he does best!

Strategies of warfare

> *Then Saul clothed David with his armor; he put a bronze helmet on his head and clothed him with a coat of mail. And David girded his sword over his armor. Then he tried to go, but could not, for he was not used to it. And David said to Saul, I cannot go with these, for I am not used to them. And David took them off.*

> —1 Samuel 17:38, 39 (AMP)

Never go to battle with weapons that are unproven! Riches, relationships, gifting, talents, and charisma are all weaponry that cannot be relied upon.

> When the strong man, fully armed, [from his courtyard] guards
> his own dwelling, his belongings are undisturbed [his property
> is at peace and is secure]. But when one stronger than he
> attacks him and conquers him, he robs him of his whole armor
> on which he had relied and divides up and distributes all his
> goods as plunder (spoil).[3]

If you are going to win the war on purity, then you mustn't rely on natural abilities alone to help you. Willpower will take you a long way, but it won't take you all the way. In addition, you have to adopt a winning strategy. He who fails to plan, plans failure.

Like every great leader in our country's most historic battles, you too must become a strategist. You must know and study your enemy, his habits, and his mode of operation. Does he attack you mostly at night or in the day? What armament does he use against you? What are the triggers he pulls? You must become relentless in your pursuit to counter his attacks and become proactive in your approach to destroy his plots against you.

Don't just fast when trouble comes, but make fasting a lifestyle. So when the attack does come, it won't take your spirit three days to figure it out. You need to be in a state of readiness at all times—a state of preparedness which allows you to call yourself to arms at a moment's notice. Being tempted is not a sin; it's a call to battle!

I recall an incident that happened to me while serving in the armed forces. My unit was on a weeklong field exercise, and it was my turn to stand watch, which lasted from midnight to 2:00 a.m. At the end of the watch, it was my responsibility to wake the soldier who was to relieve me so he could stand his leg of the watch. I decided to stand his watch for him and let him sleep instead. Everything was going well until I did the unconscionable and broke one of the eleven general orders of a sentry. I sat down while at my post. This was the last thing I remembered before being awakened by a superior officer. It was the most embarrassing moment in my entire military career.

When it comes to being vigilant, you cannot sit—not even for a moment. If you should, the enemy already has you. Even when you're tired and at the brink of giving your faith the night off, you must remain dutiful to your convictions at all times. When you become tired of watching and praying, you must reach out to those you are in covenant with so they can assist you. That night I fell asleep on my watch, I was tired and lethargic. What I should have done was wake the guy up whose duty it was to help me stand watch. Don't ever get lulled into the trap of excluding others who are there to help you accomplish your goals.

One of the biggest mistakes we make as men is not to ask others for help in time of need. We seem to have this overbearing pride or presumption that we don't need others, especially when we are coming off a high point or a major victory in our lives.

This was exactly what happened to me prior to going out on that mission. I had just been nominated for an outstanding achievement award that caused me to lean back on my laurels and be pulled into a false sense of security. Although fatigued the night I stood duty, I felt as if I could handle anything that was thrown at me. This ultimately led to poor decision making and careless behavior.

Don't ever become so overjoyed with victory that you let your guard down by resting in the triumph, instead of preparing for the next attack. The enemy will leave for a season but at some point will return to try your faith again. You must be ready and on your guard so that when the battle begins, it won't overtake you unaware.

I felt victorious, triumphant, and on top of the world prior to standing watch that night. These feelings led me to believe I didn't need the other soldier who was assigned to stand watch too.

The fact is, God never intended for us to go through anything by ourselves. No one becomes great alone. The statement which says God helps those who help themselves is not in the Bible. It sounds good, but it's bad theology. We are better together. A three-strand cord is not easily broken. When you become tired and listless in your faith, don't try to handle things on your own. Reach out to others who are there to help you maintain vigilance.

Know what you are fighting

Another strategy in winning the fight is to know what you are up against. A man took his dog to the veterinarian one day. While waiting his turn to see the doctor, he was approached by a guy who owned a pit bull. The owner of the pit bull asked if the two dogs could go out back of the hospital to fight. The other man replied, "Please, sir, I'd rather not. I just want to see the vet. I really don't want any trouble." Besides, it's wrong!

The other guy persisted by calling him names and taunting his dog as well. With that, he gave in, and they both went out back to let the dogs fight. The guy who owned the pit bull was totally caught off guard when his dog lost the fight. *This is unbelievable*, he thought as he carried his dog back into the vet's office. He couldn't believe what had just happened and began wailing about a rematch.

So out they went for round two, but this time not only did the pit bull loose, he also ended up with a badly hurt front leg. The owner of the pit bull was completely amazed and in utter disbelief. He exclaimed as he began to break down, "Man, I've never seen a dog fight like that! What kind is it?"

The other guy replied, "Well, it was an alligator before I put that fur on his back!"

You must know what you're about to fight before you engage in battle. Know what spirit is behind the attack. Whether its hatred, emulation, strife, seditions, or lust, you must understand what you are up against and learn to speak to that spirit.

Let's look, for instance, at the seducing spirits. These are spirits that work in heretical teachers, Satan's ministers, who literally teach through suggestions by demons that bring the spirit of error—for example, teachings that suggest that having sexual relations before marriage is all right as long as you love the person and have no feelings of guilt. These spirits work and operate through television, the media, radio, magazine ads, video games, phone sex, cybersex, pornography, and music videos, to name a few. The Amplified Bible translation says to "be well balanced (temperate, sober of mind), be vigilant and cautious at all times; for that enemy of yours, the devil, roams around like a lion roaring [in fierce hunger], seeking someone to seize upon and devour."[4] The devil will devour you with drugs, the occult, stealing, lying, cheating, sexual sin, and anything else you allow. Just saying no is a great slogan, but it's no match for the spiritual darkness that comes to destroy you.

A cat was crossing the road one day when its tail got knocked off by a passing car. Desperate to retrieve the tail, the cat went back onto the road, but this time, his head got knocked off, killing it instantly—not a good ending for the cat. What's the moral of the story? The moral of the story is not to lose your head over something that isn't worth it.

When you get the midnight call from that wayward girl, you cannot clip the leaves of sin. You have to deal with the root cause of the problem. First, you must not give in to the proposition or the seductive voice of the caller. Second, you must recognize the spirit behind the attack and speak to it. Call its name. The spirit of lust most assuredly is behind someone who calls you late at night and asks you to come over to their house. This is a spirit of whoredom that must be dealt with swiftly and decisively.

Pray in the following manner the next time you come under this kind of attack: "Spirit of lust, I command you to desist and decease in your maneuvers and operations against me. I prohibit you from working in this atmosphere and demand that you leave in the name of Jesus."

Keep in mind that using the name of Jesus is more than a platitude. You must have a real relationship with the Lord before the enemy will even consider your request. Remember that religion is man's attempt to reach

God; Christianity, on the other hand, is God's attempt to reach man. You need an intimate personal relationship with Jesus Christ; otherwise the adversary will not relinquish his position, and you will continue to repeat bad habits and make wrong choices.

> The weapons of our warfare are not physical [weapons of flesh and blood], but they are mighty before God for the overthrow and destruction of strongholds; [Inasmuch as we] refute arguments and theories and reasoning's and every proud and lofty thing that sets itself up against the [true] knowledge of God; and we lead every thought and purpose away captive into the obedience of Christ (the Messiah, the Anointed One).[5]

You need to understand that the weapons that are available to us are not humanly powerful but divinely powerful. The power is not ours but God's to the pulling down of strongholds. He assures us that his power will always surpass what we can do humanly. But God doesn't give us weapons to play with. He expects us to exact a strict, rigorous, and thorough attack against the enemy by taking a stand against sin. God wants us to take the initiative by being proactive rather than reacting to events. Become preemptive in your pursuit to exert force against the powers of darkness by wielding the weapons of warfare in opposition to the forces of evil.

> Finally be strong in the Lord [be empowered through your union with Him]; draw your strength from Him [that strength which His boundless might provides]. Put on God's whole armor [the armor of a heavily armed soldier which God supplies], that you may be able successfully to stand up against [all] the strategies and the deceits of the devil. For we are not wrestling with flesh and blood [contending only with physical opponents], but against the despotisms, against the powers, against [the master spirits who are] the world rulers of this present darkness, against the spirit forces of wickedness in the heavenly (supernatural) sphere. Therefore put on God's complete armor, that you may be able to resist and stand your ground on the evil day [of danger], and, having done all [the crisis demands], to stand [firmly in your place]. Stand therefore [hold your ground], having tightened the belt of truth around your loins and having put on the breastplate

of integrity and of moral rectitude and right standing with
God, and having shod your feet in preparation [to face the
enemy with the firm-footed stability, the promptness, and the
readiness produced by the good news] of the Gospel of peace.
Lift up over all the [covering] shield of saving faith, upon
which you can quench all the flaming missiles of the wicked
[one]. And take the helmet of salvation and the sword that the
Spirit wields, which is the Word of God. Pray at all times (on
every occasion, in every season) in the Spirit, with all [manner
of] prayer and entreaty. To that end keep alert and watch with
strong purpose and perseverance, interceding on behalf of all
the saints.[6]

The armor of God

The armor of God is an expression that symbolizes the combat
equipment of a Christian soldier who fights against spiritual wickedness. It
represents the full resources of God that are available to all who take up the
Cross and follow Christ. But if you are not willing to follow Christ, then
don't worry about the armor. We must "put on the *whole* armor of God"
because it's a defensive covering for the body, especially a covering (as of
metal) used in combat that affords protection.

God prepares and bestows it, but it is our responsibility to put it on.
Putting on the whole armor is a must if we are to sustain ourselves in the
battle. However, if you are not up to the fight, then you really won't need
it. It is not only our duty to put on the whole armor; it is our duty to stand
our ground and withstand the enemy at all cost.

Besides this you know what [a critical] hour this is, how it is
high time now for you to wake up out of your sleep (rouse to
reality). For salvation (final deliverance) is nearer to us now
than when we first believed (adhered to, trusted in, and relied
on Christ, the Messiah). The night is far-gone and the day is
almost here. Let us then drop (fling away) the works and deeds
of darkness and put on the [full] armor of light.[7]

Light is armor too! What happens when you turn the light on in a dark
room? Darkness has to leave. You must bring the light to every situation.

You can transform the atmosphere by shining the light of God's Word in whatever dark situation you find yourself.

The girdle of truth

> But he who practices truth [who does what is right] comes out into the Light; so that his works may be plainly shown to be what they are—wrought with God [divinely prompted, done with God's help, in dependence upon Him].

—John 3:21 (AMP)

To gird means to prepare oneself for action. The sword was suspended from the girdle, which was frequently mentioned among the articles of military dress made of leather, cloth, or cord and studded with metal plates. The doctrine of the truth should cleave to us as the girdle does to the loins, helping to restrain us from sin. Just as a girdle restrains and keeps in the body, the girdle of truth is the Christian soldier's belt that helps to prevent the Christian from doing things that may be displeasing to God.

When this foundational garment is left unemployed, most people become victim to the deception of believing falsehoods. This is usually where the spirits of error and delusion creep in and suggest something entirely different from the actual truth. These two spirits have done more to wreck the lives of men and their families than most others put together.

The spirit of error will recommend that you leave your wife and three kids for another woman who has two of her own. The spirit of delusion will convince you that you won't be happy until you do. This is one of the greatest deceptions good men buy into because they think happiness is the responsibility of their wives. Your wife is not responsible for your being happy—you are.

Furthermore, the idea that you are no longer in love with her is inspired by hell. If you believe you don't love your wife any longer, ask God to help you give to her what he has given to you, which is love unconditional, sacrificial and perfect! And then start acting like you are in love with her until real love shows up.

The breastplate

For [the Lord] put on righteousness as a breastplate.

—Isaiah 59:17 (AMP)

Righteousness must be our breastplate. The righteousness of Christ imputed to us is our breastplate against unrighteous acts of the flesh. And because we are associated with him, the righteousness that applies to him is also applied to us for we are the righteousness of God. The righteousness of Christ implanted in us is our breastplate to fortify the heart against the attacks Satan makes against us. The breastplate secures the vitals and shelters the heart.

Be well armed, man of God, as well as watchful, putting on the whole armor of God. This is necessary in order to stay sober and be prepared for the day of the Lord, because our spiritual enemies are many and mighty and malicious. They draw many to their interest and keep them in it, by making them careless, secure, and presumptuous, by making them drunk—drunk with pride, passion, self-conceit, the gratifications of illicit sexual desires, and immoralities. We need to arm ourselves against the attempts of the enemy by putting on the spiritual breastplate to keep the heart. For out of the heart spring the issues of life!

Footwear

And having shod your feet in preparation [to face the enemy with the firm-footed stability, the promptness, and the readiness produced by the good news] of the Gospel of peace.

—Ephesians 6:15 (AMP)

Shoes, or greaves of brass worn by Roman soldiers, were formerly part of the military armor used to defend the feet against the gall-traps and sharp sticks, which were laid privately in the way by the enemy to obstruct the marching. Those who were unfit to march fell upon these sharp protrusions and were wounded. The preparation of the Gospel of peace signifies a prepared and resolved frame of mind to adhere to the Gospel and abide by it; this will enable us to walk with a steady pace in the way we should go, notwithstanding the difficulties and dangers we endure as we negotiate the narrow road. It is called the Gospel of peace because it brings peace with God, with us and with others.

Having our feet shod with the preparation of the Gospel of peace will also prepare us for repentance. By living a life of repentance, we are armed against the temptation to sin.

Faith as a shield

> *Lift up over all the [covering] shield of saving faith, upon which you can quench all the flaming missiles of the wicked [one].*

> —Ephesians 6:16 (AMP)

Above anything else, we must take up the shield of faith. This is more necessary than any other armor. In the hour of temptation, faith is our all in all. The breastplate secures the vitals; but with the shield, we turn in every direction to block the attacks of the adversary. This is the victory over the world, even our faith.

We are to be fully persuaded of the truth of all God's promises and the realities that threaten our walk with Christ. Our enemy the devil is very wicked, and he strives to make us wicked as well. His temptations are called darts because of their swift flight and the immediate deep wounds they give to the soul.

Faith is the shield with which we must quench these fiery darts, rendering them ineffectual, that they may not hit us or at least not hurt us. Faith, acted upon by the Word of God together with his grace, is what quenches the fiery darts of temptation. Faith, however, will keep us observant and sober. If we believe we have spiritual enemies to wrestle with, then you must agree there is a world of spirits to prepare for. There will be times when you literally have to kneel down behind the shield of faith because of the fiery darts, which are flying, fast and furious. Faith, however, will be our best defense against the assaults of our enemies. However, if you are going to live by faith, don't expect bad news.

The helmet of salvation

And take the helmet of salvation.

—Ephesians 6:17 (AMP)

The helmet, which is the hope of salvation, protects and secures the head. A good hope of salvation, well founded and well built, will both purify the soul and keep it from being defiled by Satan, as well as comfort the soul and keep it from being troubled and tormented. Satan would tempt us to despair, but good hope keeps us trusting in God and rejoicing in him.

> But you brothers are not in [given up to the power of]
> darkness, brethren, for that day to overtake you by surprise
> like a thief. For you are all sons of light and sons of the day; we
> do not belong either to the night or to darkness. Accordingly
> then, let us not sleep, as the rest do, but let us keep wide awake
> (alert, watchful, cautious, and on our guard) and let us be
> sober (calm, collected, and circumspect). For those who sleep,
> sleep at night, and those who are drunk, get drunk at night.
> But we belong to the day; therefore, let us be sober and put on
> the breastplate of faith and love and for a helmet the hope of
> salvation.[13]

> Let us live and conduct ourselves honorably and becomingly
> as in the [open light of] day, not in reveling (carousing) and
> drunkenness, not in immorality and debauchery (sensuality
> and licentiousness), not in quarreling and jealousy. But clothe
> yourself with the Lord Jesus Christ (the Messiah), and make no
> provision for [indulging] the flesh [put a stop to thinking about
> the evil cravings of your physical nature] to [gratify its] desires
> (lusts).[14]

Watchfulness and sobriety are distinct duties and should be met with the utmost seriousness. So then do not fall asleep spiritually as others do, but let us watch; we must not be careless or indulge spiritual slothfulness and idleness. We must not be off our watch but continually upon our guard against sin and temptation to it. We must watch and act like men who are awake and stand upon their guard. We should be sober, temperate and moderate in all things. Let us keep our natural desires and appetites after the things of this world within the proper boundaries so that our hearts and minds are not overcharged with surfeiting and the cares of this world.

The Sword

> And take the sword that the Spirit exerts, which is the Word of God.

—Ephesians 6:17 (AMP)

The Word of God is the sword of the Spirit. The sword is a very necessary and useful part of a soldier's furniture. The Word of God is very necessary and of great use to the Christian in order to succeed in spiritual warfare. It is called the sword of the Spirit because of its efficacy.

> For the Word that God speaks is alive and full of power
> [making it active, operative, energizing, and effective]; it is
> sharper than any two-edged sword, penetrating to the dividing
> line of the breath of life (soul) and [the immortal] spirit, and
> of joints and marrow [of the deepest parts of our nature],
> exposing and sifting and analyzing and judging the very
> thoughts and purposes of the heart.[16]

With this we assault the assailants. Scripture arguments are the most powerful arguments to repel temptation with. Christ himself resisted Satan's temptations with "It is written, Man shall not live and be upheld and sustained by bread alone, but by every word that comes forth from the mouth of God." But the Word of God must be hidden in the heart; this helps to preserve us from sin and mortify the lusts and corruptions that are latent there.

Prayer

Pray at all times (on every occasion, in every season) in the Spirit,
with all [manner of] prayer and entreaty. To that end keep alert and
watch with strong purpose and perseverance, interceding in behalf of
all the saints (God's consecrated people).

—Ephesians 6:18 (AMP)

Prayer must buckle on all the other parts of our Christian armor. We must join prayer together with the other armament for our defense against our spiritual enemies, imploring the help and assistance of God. I really don't think that God expects us to do nothing else but pray, due to our particular stations in life that are to be done in their respective places and seasons. But we should keep up constant times of prayer, staying alert, and continually praying for all the saints. Prayer is one of the most powerful tools a Christian has available, but it's one of the least used. Prayer is vital to the level of anointing, as well as to our spiritual growth. One cannot spend time in the presence of the Lord and not be affected. Spending time in his presence will change you and supply you with the power you need to live day to day. The disciples realized the importance of prayer when they saw that Jesus prayed more than anything else, including performing miracles.

A small-town minister was asked by the board members of a very large church to consider becoming their pastor. The only catch was that he and his wife had to relocate to another city. The proposal included a new house, a new car, and a very hefty salary. That evening, when the minister talked to his wife about the matter, she asked him what his reply to the board members was. He stated that he put them off until he could think things through.

His wife became hysterical and retorted, "Think things through? Are you crazy? Didn't you hear them say a new house, a new car, and very generous compensation?"

"Yes, dear," he replied.

"Then what's the problem?" she asked.

"Well, dear, you know I like to pray about everything first before making decisions. So you go on upstairs and start packing, and I'll go in the back and pray."

As humorous as this is, many people pray in this fashion. This is the worst kind of deception. Many in the church premeditate what they want to do and then try to spiritualize it after the fact. This is not prayer. Prayer in one aspect is reciting back to God what he has already said in his Word. When you speak what God has already spoken, there is nothing more powerful than that. After all, his Word in your mouth is just as powerful as the Word in his.

Weapons of mass destruction

One of the greatest weapons in your spiritual arsenal is heaven's atomic force on the inside of you that is activated by faith and intimacy. In fact, the one thing that intimidates the enemy more than anything else is your intimacy with God. One of the greatest stratagems against his attacks is your spending time in the presence of God each day. I'm not talking about spending five minutes with him and then checking it off the list. I'm talking about spending so much time with him that we no longer see you, just him.

Faith, love, and hope are weapons too. Our hearts must become so inflamed with love for God that we become unmoved by the attacks of the enemy; this will add to our defense. True and fervent love for God will keep us attentive and non-indulgent and will hinder our backsliding in times of trouble and temptation. Faith is the key that unlocks the door to sexual purity and winning the battles that you face. Our hope of salvation helps keep us from being intoxicated with the pleasures of sin, which are but for a season. The good posture of walking in faith, love, and hope while holding onto to the responsibility of fighting the good fight is proliferated through a new level of maturity. Faith and love are always the choice of the mature, for by faith we are united to Christ and by love to our brethren.

Pleading the blood of Jesus

To know I can apply the blood of Jesus to everyday situations is awe-inspiring. As a young man growing up in the church, I did not hear a lot of emphasis placed on the blood as it relates to applying it to every circumstance in life. Instead, most of the weight was placed on using it to rebuke the enemy. I agree that can be a vital countermeasure when defending oneself against attack. But using the phrase "the blood of Jesus is against you," as if it were a magical saying or a rabbit's foot in our pockets, has little or no effect without a real relationship with Christ. Without a real relationship and true conversion of the spirit, pleading the blood of Jesus becomes nothing more than another religious practice that usually results in negative consequences when fighting the adversary. There wasn't much emphasis placed on how the blood could regulate my spiritual life. I was never taught that the blood provides. Just realizing the shed blood of Jesus has secured God's favor on my life gives me an entirely new concept of that favor. I know that when God looks at me, he sees me through the blood of Jesus that speaks on my behalf.

Chapter 5

Resisting the Enemy

So be subject to God. Resist the devil [stand firm against him], and he will flee from you.

—James 4:7 (AMP)

Allowing the Holy Spirit's control of one's whole being is a precondition to effectively resist the devil.

> Come close to God and He will come close to you. [Recognize that you are] sinners, get your soiled hands clean; [realize that you have been disloyal] wavering individuals with divided interests, and purify your hearts [of your spiritual adultery]. As you draw near to God be deeply penitent and grieve, even weep [over your disloyalty]. Let your laughter be turned to grief and your mirth to dejection and heartfelt shame [for your sins]. Humble yourselves [feeling very insignificant] in the presence of the Lord, and He will exalt you [He will lift you up and make your lives significant].[2]

"Come near to God and He will come near to you" is a clarion call to all who will defy the enemy. Simply put, it's your duty to resist, but you will not until you learn how to walk in the presence of God. You are not your own. You were bought with a price. You have an obligation and a responsibility to oppose the enemy on every front based on your covenant with God that includes security, safety, preservation, healing, assurance, and protection that is sheltered through daily confession of sin and offerings of contrition. In addition, the pursuit of silence or regular listening to the Spirit and meditation on the Word are of fundamental importance and will help you maintain integrity as you stand in opposition to the schemes of the adversary.

In resisting, you must understand that as a Christian you are not immune to Satan's attack. Why? Basically because you give him room to work in your life! On the other hand, you will never have a problem resisting the evil one while you're in the Spirit. Our hope lies in Christ's death and resurrection that defeated the adversary and makes us victorious.

> Even so consider yourselves also dead to sin and your relation
> to it broken, but alive to God [living in unbroken fellowship
> with Him] in Christ Jesus.[3]

That's why Paul went on to say that you must now start looking at yourself as one who is "alive unto God through Jesus Christ our Lord." You see, sin is no longer your master now that you are the servant of Jesus Christ! When your body, mind, and emotions are submitted to him, you cease to be a slave to them. Instead, your body, mind, and emotions become your servant and instruments of righteousness to help you achieve the dreams that God has put in your heart. Ask the Holy Spirit to energize you with strength and the ability to walk in the resurrection power of Jesus Christ. God will send strength to your situation when you say yes to his will. Obedience gives birth to results.

If you want positive results in resisting, then start obeying and stop putting difficulties into your destiny. Stop letting the way you live complicate the purpose of God for your life. Learn how to praise until your flesh concedes. Let your praise come before pressure instead of praising after pressure comes. When you praise because of problems that come your way, usually that praise is a token. The real praise doesn't come until the other side of the problem.

Don't just get broken because of problems. Allow God to break you through communion. You should expect that if you break bread with him, then he will break you—he will break your will to sit on the throne of your own heart, thus giving him complete control, which will ultimately help you resist the enemy and give you complete victory.

Chapter 6

Overcoming Temptation

Let no one say when he is tempted, I am tempted of God; for God is incapable of being tempted by [what is] evil and He Himself tempts no one. But every person is tempted when he is drawn away, enticed and baited by his own evil desire (lust, passions). Then the evil desire, when it has conceived, gives birth to sin, and sin, when it is fully matured, brings forth death.

—James 1:13 (AMP)

When lust overtakes you and immorality gets in the way of your devotion to Christ, you must give priority to the things that lead you back to him. Otherwise you will keep alive the reckless behavior of your flesh and continue the insanity of doing the same things while expecting different outcomes.

We live in a day where temptation lurks behind every corner, waiting on those who are less discerning, caring, and vigilant. What does the enemy use against you to keep you in a state of spiritual unrest? What's your trap? What causes the inclinations that you detest to remain in your life?

You can always tell when a person's life is filled with God. They are the ones who make statements regarding faith without opening their mouths. I believe, the reason so many men fall to wanton desires is that they don't have a true relationship with God. What they have is religion, which becomes easily disregarded when it comes to taking a stand against carnality and the requirements of the flesh. It's impossible for your life to be filled with God if your heart is not filled with God. Your ability to say no to sin depends on your allegiance and the depth of your love for Christ. Jesus said, "If you love me, then keep my commandments."

Many in the body of Christ fall into the trap of just looking or acting spiritual rather than spending quality time in his presence, which develops a deeper commitment to him. Going to church for a couple of hours on Sunday hardly constitutes a meaningful relationship. You wouldn't accept it if your wife only spoke to you one day out of the week or just when she wanted something from you. So then why do it to God? Why go through the motions of serving him without real transformation? If you really want to change and not just settle for the substitutes of the world, then you must meet Jesus at the well of life, where he will give you living water.

Oftentimes, as men, we allow our prime biological functions to dictate our desires and our obsessive fixation on the opposite sex, which is where the problem with temptation comes in. Due to our inability to possess our vessels with sanctification and honor, we often succumb to the primary need to engage in sexual intercourse, which is not the problem. After all, God created us with the urge to have sex within the confines of marriage. The problem is with not learning how to exercise restraint. If sex were a holiday, for most men it would be the Fourth of July every day of the week, complete with sparkles and fireworks. Herein lies the problem for most couples: he wants sex too much, and she doesn't want it enough, which is one reason so many homes are miserably unhappy and in despair.

Sex was given as the ultimate demonstration of love between a married man and woman. So important is it to a healthy marriage that God commands us not to defraud one another. If she says those four words every husband dreads hearing, "I have a headache," you must remain the gentleman you are and not pressure her into giving in—even if it means you biting the bedpost throughout the night, give her the rest and respect she deserves. I guarantee it will yield benefits that will pay the sweetest delights. The next time you get that feeling, offer her an aspirin before bedtime. When she asks, "What's that for? I don't have a headache," just reply, "I'm glad to hear it, honey" and turn out the lights.

But seriously, a Christian marriage is a spiritual union with God that is intended to be a visible expression of his love. The adversary, however, in his attempt to destroy the church, has made an all-out onslaught against the family. He has attacked the family on every front, especially in the area of sexual fulfillment. Couple that with an already volatile marital situation and you could very well become tempted to step outside of the will of God concerning your vows of fidelity.

The solution is not to make provision for the flesh to fulfill the lust thereof—that is, viewing pornography. It should be stated that viewing sexually explicit material reduces the fulfillment of sex within the marriage to less of a meaningful experience and robs us of the intimacy and happiness we so affectionately long for. Men become distracted instead of enriched by the images of pornography, which leads to relational degradation between husbands and wives. As men, what do we expect our wives to look like after we've viewed porn? How can we expect them to compete with the images etched into our subconscious minds?

Contrary to the popular belief, watching pornography doesn't promote a deeper, richer experience with each other. People who think that it enhances their relationship are deceived. If the woman picks out a movie that has porn in it most of the time, it's boring with too much plot for the man, but he goes along with it because he thinks she wants it. She primarily goes along with it in anticipation of developing greater emotional support from him, something she yearns for. The irony is, when she can no longer satisfy his sexual fantasies, he then begins to explore other outlets to fulfill his insatiable appetite, such as cybersex or developing other relationships outside of the marriage. In a survey done by the American Academy of Matrimonial Lawyers, more than half said that the Internet has played a "significant role" in divorces and that online porn lead to half of these cases.

Christianity, however, counterbalances the destructive cultural messages pornography sends and helps to overcome the stark realities of social corruption that relate to institutions, whose interests lie in desensitizing mainstream civilization from the Judeo-Christian beliefs.

To win the battle over pornography, you must become cognizant of the fact that there are ungodly forces, both natural and spiritual, that influence us on subliminal levels. In our attempt to overcome temptation, it is very important to discern these influences, as well as understand the concealed messages that try to manipulate our minds. In doing so, you will be able to understand more completely when the enemy tries to attack you through your thought process.

Three distinct voices regulate our decisions. The first and most significant authority is the voice of God. It should be stated, however, that God's voice is often obscured by our own innate thoughts, which is the second voice that has power over a lot of the choices that we make. The last and most surreptitious of the three is the voice of the adversary, who very deceitfully transfers his thoughts to us by making us believe his thoughts are our own, therefore exacting his will upon us without any sound judgment on our part whatsoever. Thoughtful consideration of this will dramatically reduce your propensity to relapse.

We yield to temptation partly because of the voice of enticement we so often listen to that goes unquestioned. We simply don't grasp who's behind the command for us to give in. And because the thoughts go unchallenged, we make decisions that are tied to learned behaviors and underlying issues in our lives. In essence, we contemplate and make choices based on our own carnalities when we pray, "Lord, deliver me—just not tonight!"

There are, however, consequences of sin. For every action there is a reaction. The one who sows to please his sinful nature, from that nature will reap destruction; the one who sows to please the Spirit, from the Spirit will reap eternal life. You will ultimately reap what you sow. Your flesh reaps corruption, but the one who sows to the Spirit shall of the Spirit reap everlasting life. Sin starts with fascination, transitions to visualization, and ends with the act.

Satan whispered to Eve, "For God knows that in the day you eat of it your eyes will be opened and you will be like God, knowing the difference between good and evil and blessing and calamity. And when the woman saw that the tree was good (suitable, pleasant) for food and that it was delightful to look at, and a tree to be desired in order to make one wise, she took of its fruit and ate; and she gave some also to her husband, and he ate."[2]

There is nothing quite like the intoxicating effects and fascination of having something that doesn't belong to you, especially in the area of sexuality. Once the fascination is conceived, it then moves to the realm of sin, which is better understood as the tangible aspects or the reward of one's immorality. This ultimately leads to carrying out the act in disobedience to God. Adam, who I believe was standing there and should have protected his wife, did not face trouble like a man; instead, when it was all said and done, he blamed Eve.

Justification will never excuse you from doing the will of God. Simply because the will of God is not predicated upon what someone else will or will not do! You cannot justify using pornography because your wife doesn't have sex with you as often as you would like. Even if she uses sex as leverage to obtain something she wants, it's still no excuse. In situations like this, you must allow the Holy Spirit to minister to you so you can maintain your duties as the priest of your home. Otherwise, you will give in to temptation and act out certain behaviors to get what you feel is rightfully yours.

You must allow the Holy Spirit to change your wife, which you have mistaken to be your duty. You cannot change her; this will only lead to added frustration. Your job is to love her. You are the caregiver; the Holy Spirit is the cure-giver. He will bring her to the truth and knowledge of his Word concerning areas that are misaligned in her life. You must be patient and allow the Holy Spirit to produce the fruit in her that she is capable of yielding. It won't always be easy, but the process will go a lot smoother if you walk in love and allow God to use you as a sacrifice of his grace.

Temptations trap

> *In the spring, when kings go forth to battle, David sent Joab with his servants and all Israel, and they ravaged the Ammonites [country] and besieged Rabbah. But David remained in Jerusalem. One evening David arose from his couch and was walking on the roof of the king's house, when from there he saw a woman bathing; and she was very lovely to behold. David sent and inquired about the woman. One said, Is not this Bathsheba, the daughter of Eliam and the wife of Uriah the Hittite? And David sent messengers and took her. And she came in to him, and he slept with her—for she was purified from her uncleanness. Then she returned to her house.*

> —2 Samuel 11:1-4 (AMP)

Restlessness and dissatisfaction are environments that are always associated with sin. What is the environment you live in made of? What are you watching, listening to, or involved in? You must create an atmosphere for the Holy Spirit to reside in. You must become more responsible for what you see, hear, and say, as well as whom you allow to influence you. Godly associations will bring blessings, while ungodly associations will corrupt good behavior.

In simplest terms, King David created an environment that led to his fall with Bathsheba. He was out of position and had no business being in Jerusalem during that time. Instead, he should have been with the other men of God doing the will of God. David gave his faith a holiday and decided to flesh out.

When you decide to stay home from church with hopes of getting rest, the fact is you never really rest. Instead, the enemy will disquiet your spirit and give you unrest, which, left to its own misguidance, will often lead to sin.

Notice what happened to David. First, he was at home when he should have been cooperating with the will of God and other believers. Second, he became restless. Third, he was tempted. Last, he fell to the temptation. I will say on David's behalf, unlike many men in the body of Christ, he knew the difference between true repentance and just saying, "I'm sorry."

Closer examination of David and his relationship with God will prove he was perhaps one of the greatest kings of Israel and one of the most prominent figures in the history of the Jewish people. He was an athlete from his youth, a fine musician, and a poetic genius. He wrote some of the greatest masterpieces of spiritual literature of that time. In addition, a large number of the psalms are credited to him. He was an able general who conducted his military campaigns with great success. David was a man after God's own heart and by far one of the most famous ancestors of Christ. Jesus is not called the Son of Abraham or the Son of Jacob but the Son of David. Even through failure David knew by maintaining a real relationship with God, he could get his prayers answered. Let's examine the things David did that led to failure.

He forsook the assembling together with other believers.

> Do not forsake or neglecting to assemble together [as believers],
> as is the habit of some people, but admonishing (warning,
> urging, and encouraging) one another, and all the more
> faithfully as you see the day approaching.[4]

Some people asked if they could stay home from church and still receive the corporate blessings reserved for those in attendance. My reply was an unequivocal yes! There are those who are bedridden and sick and cannot physically attend church on a routine basis. God understands that. Then there are those who stay home because they just don't feel like going. They often experience what I consider to be an identity and energy crisis. They forget who they are and don't have enough energy to find out!

Not going to church is like watching a football game on your television set at home. When your team scores, you can scream, shout, and get excited at home just like those who are actually at the game. But there is nothing like being at the stadium with others who are there to support your team, particularly when your team scores a touchdown. The impetus of praise and worship can be experienced alone, but the magnitude of being in his presence with other believers is far reaching and in many cases unsurpassed.

He became slothful in service, which led to his becoming restless.

> As the door turns on its hinges, so does the lazy man [move not
> from his place] upon his bed.[5]

As men of faith, we were designed to worship; when we fail to maintain our allegiances in service to God, we then develop other alliances, usually to our flesh, which drives us in becoming obstinate or unwilling to be guided or controlled.

He coveted that which did not belong to him. In due course, this led to many sorrows.

> You shall not covet your neighbor's house, your neighbor's wife,
> or his manservant, or his maidservant, or his ox, or his donkey,
> or anything that is your neighbor's.[6]

He also did several things that led to his rise.

First, he uncovered his wrongdoings.

> For I am conscious of my transgressions and I acknowledge
> them; my sin is ever before me.[7]

> He who covers his transgressions will not prosper, but whoever
> confesses and forsakes his sins will obtain mercy.[8]

Second, he confessed his sin.

> Against You, You only, have I sinned and done that which is
> evil in your sight, so that you are justified in your sentence and
> faultless in your judgment.[9]

> If we [freely] admit that we have sinned and confess our sins,
> He is faithful and just (true to His own nature and promises)
> and will forgive our sins [dismiss our lawlessness] and
> [continuously] cleanse us from all unrighteousness [everything

not in conformity to His will in purpose, thought, and
action].[10]

Last, he repented.

> Have mercy upon me, O God, according to your steadfast
> love; according to the multitude of your tender mercy and
> loving-kindness blot out my transgressions.[11]

Psalm 51 was David's prayer for the remission of his sins and for his
sanctification. It is imperative you learn how to use the power of intimacy
with Christ so you can overcome the things that easily overwhelm you.
The solution to this is to learn how to live on higher spiritual levels. This
means to consider making decisions based on the Word of God, which you
must believe to be infallible and incapable of error. To the degree you learn
to value the Word of God, is the degree to which you will begin to make
quality godly decisions and triumph over the lure of sin.

The more value we place on something, the more we cherish it. You
must understand that the level of superior decision making regarding
overcoming temptation is directly proportionate to the value we place on
the Word of God. Low esteem of the Word will produce poor choices.
High esteem of the Word will produce godly choices.

God does not operate on a hit-or-miss basis, and he doesn't expect us
to either. The Word was given to us as a model so we would know how
to conduct our lives on a daily basis. The only way to truly make good
decisions regarding our present or future behavior is to value the Word,
cherishing it as though your very life depended upon it. Living on this level
requires us to look at every aspect our lives from the standpoint of what
God desires and what brings honor to him.

Once the covert operation of the enemy is exposed, dealing with the
obstacles that prevent you from walking with God daily is the next step to
recovery. Fear, past failures, and pride are obstacles that must be eradicated
before the healing process can begin.

In my opinion, fear is the most crippling of the three impediments
and the one that will most likely be used against you. The Holy Spirit is so
adamant regarding fear that he gave us sixty-two verses that tell us to fear
not. Fear is a barrier that will keep you from your breakthrough and is very
crippling because it shuts down any hope of getting set free from the power
of any sin, for example, pornography.

How then do you deal with fear (false evidence appearing real)? The spirit of fear must be dealt with by using the Word of God to combat all its forces. Fear looks at the Goliath of impurity and says, "He's too big to hit," while faith, which is the opposite of fear, looks at the giant and says, "He's too big to miss." The important thing about defeating the enemy is never to run mutely at the giant. When David slew Goliath, he ran at the giant speaking to it. You must speak the Word if you are to become victorious in your pursuit for freedom over the obstacles in your life.

Past failures are akin to the spirit of fear and are adhesives that tie us to the negative thinking of our past and earlier periods of failure in our lives. The very fact that you have failed over and over again ignites the memories of past failures and urges you to give up. Some have fallen so many times that they simply refuse to believe they can be set free. It doesn't matter to God how many times you've failed at your attempt to become pure; he doesn't count! What matters to him is your victory. The greater the fight, the greater the victory! In the end, God will redeem the years of pain and struggle by allowing your life to become a witness of his grace, mercy, and resurrection power.

In his writings, Apostle Paul exhorts the Philippians to forget the things that are behind. Looking back is sure to end in going back. Living in the past will always rob us of our God-given potential, and unregenerate thinking will always stop success by holding us captive to the harmful periods of our lives. Therefore, we must not allow our past failures to determine our future successes. The Lord didn't see Peter in his problem; he saw Peter in his potential. God is not concerned with who you are, inasmuch as he's concerned with who you are becoming. Where you are going is far more important than where you have been.

Pride is the most sinister of the three impediments because its secret nature often lurks behind the shadows of religious thinking, which causes some to consent to the idea that everyone else has a problem except for them. This further complicates matters and precludes them from getting the help they so desperately need. To put it in simplest terms, pride would rather you just look like a well of living water than to become filled with his Spirit so others can drink from your life.

I believe that any level of success regarding purity is commensurate with one's ability to eradicate pride. It is only when we humble ourselves and admit that we need help are we in a position to truly be set free by God.

When you resist the Holy Spirit and fail to yield to his influence, it grieves the Father. When you give your faith time off, you become victim to the vices of your flesh. You must not be distracted from the forward momentum of your faith. Make your heart a home for the Holy Spirit to dwell in instead of a hotel where he has to check out in the morning. Learn to practice his presence, which means to live life with the awareness that he is always with you no matter what. Learn to venerate his presence. His love for you is matchless! He will see you through the things you do and love you too. His grace is sufficient for you, no matter how many times you fall. That's not important. What is important to God is getting back up.

When my son was just learning to walk, he would constantly fall down. When he would fall, I would rush to his aid, pick him up, and set him on his way again. It didn't matter how many times he fell. The outcome of my love never changed. I would always rush to his side to sustain him. Not once did I say to my wife, "If that kid falls one more time, I'm kicking him out of the house." When he falls, he is still my son. I did, however, look forward with great anticipation to the day he wouldn't fall. Why? I simply didn't want him to get hurt.

Do you realize that your heavenly Father is incapable of loving you any more or any less than he loves you right now? His love for you is not based on your performance. It's based on the immutable power of his Word. It's not based on what you do; it's based on who he is. You cannot affect his love, but you can affect his favor. When you fall, you must get up and run to the arms of Jesus as he will pick you up and carry you to the Father's heart. If you do not depend on him when you fall, on whom do you depend? On what do you depend? Learn to depend on Jesus.

To be filled with the Spirit of God is the key to overcoming temptation. You can try to overcome by your own strength, but in the final analysis, you are going to need Jesus. Overcoming temptation is not automatic. Even though the price is paid and we are released from the stronghold of sin through the emancipation of his blood, we still have to respond to the Word before winning over the enticements of the flesh. Jesus shed his blood for you, but you are not going to be truly successful and victorious until you acknowledge Christ and receive him as your Savior.

I can tell you categorically whose lives will be changed after reading this book and whose won't. The lives that will be transformed are those with enough faith to take these truths and apply them. The principles stated here will work in any situation in which they are applied. So then you will receive from God only what you believe him for. The question is not "What can God do?" The question is "What can you believe? What can you believe God for in your life, finances, health, your relationships, and your marriage?" The fact is, God is ready to bless you right now!

It is not that most Christians want to behave inappropriately; we simply do because of unresolved inner turmoil, unresolved inner conflicts and baggage from our past. What am I saying? I'm saying you have to get to the root cause of your problems. You have to get rid of the baggage that separates you from God. You can clip the leaves of sin and remedy the problem temporarily—like cutting a lawn full of dandelions. The yard looks good for a while, but soon the problem returns because you didn't destroy the root. What is the root cause of your problem?

Let's take lying as a problem we want to solve. Imagine that one of your children is a habitual liar. What is the source or the motivating factor of people who lie? There are many reasons why people lie, but most assuredly, fear is the root cause. Fear motivates lying because the person not telling the truth would rather lie than disappoint those to whom they must answer. In order to wash your hands of whatever problem you face, you must go to the source of the difficulty and not just skim over the shallow portions of your dilemmas.

How to overcome

Stir up the fallow ground.

—Hosea 10:12 (AMP)

You must stir up the fallow ground so the Word can penetrate your heart. (*Fallow ground* in the Greek is *ground already plowed,* but because it sat dormant too long, it became encrusted over.) Any ground in this state is incapable of receiving seed and needs to be plowed again if it is going to produce fruit.

Renew your mind. The significant problems you face cannot be solved at the same level of thinking where you were when the problem was created.

Become transformed by the renewing of your mind so you may
prove what is that good, and acceptable, and perfect will of
God. (Rom. 12:2)

In other words, "Fill your mind with the Word of God."

Make God a priority in your life. Put him first, your mate second, and yourself last.

> Commit your way to the Lord [roll and repose each care of
> your load on Him]; trust (lean on, rely on, and be confident)
> also in Him and He will bring it to pass.[12]

Commitment is not a contract; it is an act of the will. A contract says, "I can get out if it doesn't work." Everyone has problems. Good people as well as bad face the same problems; the difference is one of commitment. Commitment is synonymous with covenant, which in the Old Testament always required a sacrifice. Commitment says, "I will sacrifice myself for the cause of Christ."

Each day we arise, we must ask the Lord to meet us at the place where we willingly crucify our flesh on the Cross. Learn to build character that helps to activate God's power in your life. Develop a disdain for sin.

> Do not love or cherish the world or the things that are in the
> world. If anyone loves the world, love for the Father is not in
> him. For all that is in the world—the lust of the flesh [craving
> for sensual gratification] and the lust of the eyes [greedy
> longings of the mind] and the pride of life [assurance in one's
> own resources or in the stability of earthly things]—these do
> not come from the Father but are from the world [itself].[13]

> You [are like] unfaithful wives [having illicit love affairs with
> the world and breaking your marriage vow to God]! Do you
> not know that being the world's friend is being God's enemy?
> So whoever chooses to be a friend of the world takes his stand
> as an enemy of God.[14]

> For whatever is born of God is victorious over the world; and
> this is the victory that conquers the world, even our faith.
> Who is it that is victorious over [that conquers] the world but
> he who believes that Jesus is the Son of God [who adheres to,
> trusts in, and relies on that fact]?[15]

"You are an overcomer." You've got to get this in your "new-mah," which is your spirit, not just in your "su-kay," which is your soul and mind, so your "so-mah" or physical man will fall in line with your spirit-man. Your mind does not have the capacity to understand God. You need your spirit to cooperate with him. Develop and exercise your spirit so that heaven can open up over your life.

The spirit is what communicates with God. If you ever learn to listen to the Spirit of God with your spirit, then all your problems will be solved. You're still going to have challenges, but you'll have victories too. The real you is a spirit. Speak from there. This is where power is released.

Meditate on the Word daily. Stay close to the Lord through communion and fellowship. Walk in truth and love. And should you fall, repent.

Learn to partner with God, spirit to Spirit.

> Strip yourselves of your former nature [put off and discard your
> old un-renewed self] which characterized your previous manner
> of life and becomes corrupt through lusts and desires that
> spring from delusion; and be constantly renewed in the spirit of
> your mind [having a fresh mental and spiritual attitude].[16]

Chapter 7

After a Fall

For a righteous man falleth seven times, and riseth up again.

—Proverbs 24:16 (AMP)

A man is not finished when he falls; he's finished when he quits! You are not a failure when you fall, but you must not stay in that position. You must get up, repent, turn from sin, and get back into fellowship with the Lord. The road to purity is a marathon, not a sprint. It is a lifelong race that must be met with patience and endurance. To run the Christian race with patience means to run with steadfast perseverance. It means to run the race with determination and fortitude so that we are stirred to run the whole race, casting away all hindrances while looking to Jesus, who is our supreme example and the author and finisher of our faith. Running to win is finishing the course.

Have you ever been in a place where you've asked yourself whether it is worth it to go the whole way? Then I ask you, "Is your wife worth your going the whole way? Are your kids worth it? How about your personal ministry?" You are not running this race for yourself; you are running it for them too. So stay in the race! And should you experience a fall along the way, there's only one option—get up!

True recovery, however, should begin with the inner part, but man often cleans up the outside, making no change or modification on the inside. To pretend you are spiritually well when you aren't is the worst kind of concealment.

First of all, it doesn't bring about true change. It also allows the enemy to perpetrate the lie that you are incapable of overcoming your problems. It also causes you to take the position that you will never measure up to others, especially to those who may be further along in their walk with the Lord. Don't ever compare yourself with others, particularly the sprinters. The race is not given to the swift or to the strong but to the one who endures to the end. You must run your own race with patience, realizing that you are never beyond the reach of God's love and forgiveness.

Lives cannot be so shattered or torn apart that the power of God can't put them back together again. With God all things are possible, if you only believe. God is not standing by waiting to hit you over the head every time you make a mistake, but he does want you to overcome the things that keep you from having a deeper relationship with him.

At some point, you must grow beyond falling to the same old things. Your love for God must take priority over your love for the things that cause you to decrease. When you willfully choose the path of sin, when you choose your flesh over your faith, you prolong the inevitability of who you're called to be.

A pastor and friend of mine would often say, "We were created and we fell." We were redeemed, but we live carnal. We feed our flesh three hot meals a day and our spirit one cold snack a week!

There is a cure, however, for the maladies that plague our lives, a cure for passionless living, confused thinking, and double-mindedness. There is a cure for wavering, lack of trust, hatred and strife, lethargy, and powerless religion. There is a cure for marital failure, addictions, infidelity, and, yes, even divorce. If you can obtain this one thing, it will be a panacea for every hurt and shortfall in your life. It will restore your soul, ignite fresh passion, desire, and vision, and fill you with unspeakable joy so you become freshly anointed to pursue and fulfill the passion for which you were ultimately designed, which is to live with the person and in the presence of God who made you.

David realized every answer he sought, for all his problems had to begin with following one desire:

> That I may dwell in the house of the Lord [in His presence] all
> the days of my life, to behold and gaze upon the beauty [the
> sweet attractiveness and the delightful loveliness] of the Lord
> and to meditate, consider, and inquire in His temple.[2]

The secret to not falling willfully is to know God and to set aside time for him every day so that you can share his life, touch his heart, and have him touch yours, realizing that in and of yourself you do not have the capacity to be content. We were created to depend on one person and one person only—the man Christ Jesus. It's never too late to return to the Lord. It's not over for you; it's just beginning. The rest of your life is the best of your life! So position yourself firmly in the freedom wherewith Christ has made you free and be not enslaved again with the workings of darkness. And should you become enticed, do not give in.

Learn to separate yourself from the toxic things in your life.

> Now to Him who is able to keep you without stumbling or
> slipping or falling, and to present [you] unblemished (blameless
> and faultless) before the presence of His glory in triumphant
> joy and exultation [with unspeakable, ecstatic delight].[3]

Practical steps that you can take

Relinquish the position of setting the security levels on the Internet. Setting the security measures on your computer is no longer your responsibility. At the very least, your wife should set and maintain all security measures, as well as control the master screen name on the account. You are fooling yourself if you think you are capable of exercising the proper security measures to maintain compliance.

Change the atmosphere when you're being tempted. Don't stay in harm's way by staying in the environment. To think that you are in control of a potentially hazardous situation without changing the atmosphere is naive at best. We know from basic fire-fighting procedures that if we remove the energy that fuels the fire, it will go out. Changing the environment for some involves removing one or more of the elements. Sometimes the fire is so hot that we cannot extinguish it without the help of others.

There will be times, however, when we simply cannot find someone to pray us through. In this scenario, we would remove the oxygen that fuels the fire, which in this case would be ourselves. At times like these, you must literally leave the surrounding influences as quickly as possible. If you are spiritually incapable of extinguishing the fires of temptation, then you must change your posture. You must get out of the house or that place immediately! A good run is better than a poor fight any day of the week.

Take control of your thoughts. You can't stop a bird from flying over your head, but you don't have to let it build a nest in your hair. To overcome bad thoughts that plague your mind, you must first renew your mind as the Word tells us to do. You must begin to systematically replace the lewd material you view, listen to, and read with the Word of God.

Here's an exercise to illustrate how to take control of bad thoughts that come into your mind. Try counting to ten silently, and when you get to five, say your name out loud. What happened when you spoke? You stopped counting. It is literally impossible for the subconscious mind to do both at the same time. The same principle applies to your spirit as well. When bad thoughts come into your mind, take these negative thoughts captive through praise. Praise and bad thoughts cannot occupy the same realm simultaneously.

Become more accountable. Accountability must go beyond just giving someone a progress report each Sunday morning when you see him or her at church. The next level of accountability is to have your accountability partner view what you're viewing on the Internet by using tracking software that's available online. If you are not willing to be transparent with your accountability partner, then you are not ready for true accountability.

Focus. Justification is the reason for our lack of focus. If you continue to justify your wrongdoings, then your ability to focus will be greatly diminished. In addition, your capacity to concentrate on winning over your flesh is absolutely critical to your continued success. You cannot afford to become lackadaisical regarding your pursuit to remain pure. You must become more aware of the little foxes that spoil the nest. Something as simple as a magazine that comes in the mail can be enough to offset your focus. If you can't look through the ladies section of a Sears catalogue without having impure thoughts or actions, then you don't need to look! Billboards that promote sex can be detrimental to your ability to control the triggers that visually stimulate you. Discipline yourself to look the other way. The next time your eyes are tempted, say these words out loud: Don't Look! Exercising restraint along with your ability to regulate control is vital. True disciplined people are disciplined from the inside out, not the outside in. They are not subject to external things.

Covenant prayer: Dear heavenly Father, more than anything else I want my relationship with you to have first place in my life. I now trust you to meet my need for love and acceptance, and so I give my life to you afresh. I ask for your wisdom and guidance concerning my relations with others as I take a stand for you. Lord, I want your best for my life. Please help me to be strong and not ever compromise my stand to remain pure. Thank you for your Word, and how it gives me life and the direction I need! In Jesus's name I pray.

Chapter 8

How to Escape

For no temptation (no trial regarded as enticing to sin), [no matter how it comes or where it leads] has overtaken you and laid hold on you that is not common to man [that is, no temptation or trial has come to you that is beyond human resistance and that is not adjusted and adapted and belonging to human experience, and such as man can bear]. But God is faithful [to His Word and to His compassionate nature], and He [can be trusted] not to let you be tempted and tried and assayed beyond your ability and strength of resistance and power to endure, but with the temptation He will [always] also provide the way out (the means of escape to a landing place), that you may be capable and strong and powerful to bear up under it patiently.

—1 Corinthians 10:13 (AMP)

I went to the grocery store one day, and while I was there, a young woman propositioned me. She began to tell me what she wanted to do with me and waited for my reply. I was shocked by her forward behavior and hadn't told her of my faith before exclaiming to her that I was married. She then looked at me with a facial expression that would make a sailor blush and said, "Bring your wife too!" At that point, it didn't pay for me to say anything further. I simply turned in the opposite direction and left the store. In retrospect, when a proposition of this sort comes to you, you are not under any obligation to speak to the person unless you are casting that spirit out. For most of us, this simply means we will turn and take flight before the enemy affronts us.

The Scripture says, "There hath no temptation taken you but such as is common to man: but God is faithful, who will not suffer you to be tempted above that ye are able; but will with the temptation also make a way to escape, that ye may be able to bear" (1 Cor. 10:13). The Word is very concise and to the point. God will always give you a way out, but you must take it.

It is not so for the young Christian who fell into sin because of his inability to recognize an attack. A young lady he worked with asked him if he wanted to come over to her house one evening to watch a pay-per-view fight. Apparently, she had invited a few other guests over as well. Or so he thought! Not suspecting anything amiss, he agreed.

The peculiar thing about the arrangement was that he was assigned the task of letting the others in as they arrived. Apparently, she had to work late the evening of the fight and was afraid she might not get home in time to let her guests in. No problem. He took her house key and later that evening went over and waited for the others to arrive. When the prefight started and no one else showed up, he became a little concerned but figured that they would no doubt be there for the main event.

Well, no one else showed up to watch the fight, and eventually the young lady came home. It was quite late, and the fight was over. When asked about the others who never showed, the young lady responded, "Oh yea, they cancelled at the last moment!"

That was his first sign to leave. Instead, he complied with her plea to remain seated while she slipped into something more comfortable (second sign). She served him an intoxicating drink and turned on sin-a-max (third sign). I will spare you the details of this young man's fall, but you can clearly see how this was a demonic setup from the very beginning.

The Word of God teaches us to possess our vessels with sanctification and honor. My advice would be not to get into situations you have to get out of. Don't set yourself up for a fall, and most certainly, do not go back to look further.

> Now that you have come to be acquainted with and understand
> and know [the true] God, or rather to be understood and
> known by God, how can you turn back again to the weak and
> beggarly and worthless elementary things [of all religions before
> Christ came], whose slaves you once more want to become?[2]

When you chain a baby elephant to a post in the ground, it will at first try to escape. The animal at this age is simply no match for the shackles, which prohibit its escape. Ironically, at some point, it gives up the struggle and succumbs to the insignificant metal stake as its master. After years of conditioning and inverted thinking, the elephant, now fully grown, no longer comprehends its immense power or its ability to break the chain that restrains him like a thin piece of thread. Instead, it remains satisfied with the partnership of this inanimate object that now has full control.

Many great men are in this same condition. Programmed by years of struggle and defeat, they simply become brainwashed into thinking they are powerless over the things, which limits their freedom.

> Therefore since we are surrounded by so great a cloud of witnesses [who have borne testimony to the Truth], let us strip off and throw aside every encumbrance (unnecessary weight) and that sin which so readily (deftly and cleverly) clings to and entangles us, and let us run with patient endurance and steady and active persistence the appointed course of the race that is set before us.[3]

This is an exhortation to be constant and persevere. The sin that so easily besets us is that sin to which we are most prone or vulnerable. It is that to which we are most exposed from habit, age, or circumstance. It is very important that this scripture passage becomes more than a slogan or catch phrase when dealing with the things with which you struggle. Whatever causes you to fall must be challenged, faced, and corrected. For whatever a man's secret sin is, be it what it will, as long as it remains unrestrained, will hinder him from living a life of virtue, as sin takes from him every motive for living pure, giving power to every discouragement.

When you become weary and faint in your spirit, recollect that Jesus suffered to save you from every sin imaginable. After all, what are our trials compared to the agonies he suffered at the Cross? What are they to the sufferings of our Lord? One of the quickest escape routes from temptation is to visit *praise.com*, the place where you come out with your hands up and fight the battle through praise. This is where you take Judah to the fight! Remember, Judah was the tribe that led the processional with song and dance unto the Lord as they marched into battle.

You may feel at times that you're not able to get your prayers up, but you can certainly bring heaven down to your circumstance through praise and worship. Remember, faith moves mountains, but praise moves God. The Lord said that he inhabits the praises of his people. If you think about it, there are only two times to praise the Lord: when you feel like it, and when you don't!

Chapter 9

Reaching Your Potential

Jesus answered him, If you would be perfect [that is, have that spiritual maturity which accompanies self-sacrificing character], go and sell what you have and give to the poor, and you will have riches in heaven; and come, be my disciple [side with my party and follow me]. But when the young man heard this, he went away sad (grieved and in much distress), for he had great possessions.

—Matthew 19:21, 22 (AMP)

And Jacob was left alone, and a Man wrestled with him until daybreak. And when he saw that he prevailed not against him, he touched the hollow of his thigh; and the hollow of Jacob's thigh was out of joint, as he wrestled with him. And he said, let me go, for the day breaketh. And he said I will not let thee go, except thou bless me. And he said unto him, what [is] thy name? And he said, Jacob. And he said, Thy name shall be called no more Jacob, but Israel: for as a prince hast thou power with God and with men, and hast prevailed.

—Genesis 32:24-28 (AMP)

Wrestling, as Jacob did, would disqualify a lot of people nowadays because at midnight their flesh would say that's enough. Some things you will never receive until you learn to wrestle all night long through prayer and fasting. Notice the three important things that happened to Jacob. He never walked

74

the same; he got a new name and was given power with God and man. Needless to say, Jacob's perseverance that night propelled him into Jewish history as one of the great patriarchs of that nation. Sadly enough, some will never reach their full potential, never realize their purpose in life, and never step into public ministry because they are not willing to wrestle for their future or fight to step out of private sin.

If you desire to be perfect, that is, to be a real Christian, if you want to reach your highest potential and do all that God has designed for you to do, *then you must sell out yourself to Christ.* This means getting rid of everything that separates you from following Him! The Lord, who reads the hearts of men, knew that the rich young ruler's inner sin was the love of the world. Jesus could see that he had made a god of his possessions and that his love for material things was keeping him from following Jesus. The young man went away, not willing to have salvation at so high a price.

What is reaching your potential in Christ worth? You were created because God wants something to be done that demands your existence. You were created with inherent inclinations, talents, and gifts to fulfill the will of God. Finding God's purpose for your life is the key to reaching your ability. You must find your hidden talents, discover your passions, and embrace them with all your heart. If you are willing to submit and work together with God, then nothing will be impossible for you.

You are losing battles because you're not yielding to him. The likelihood of your becoming what God has designed for your life is contingent upon your willingness to submit and yield to his authority. If you are willing to surrender your will in exchange for his, then, and only then, will you begin to walk into the purpose God has for your life.

Enemies of your potential

In his book entitled Maximizing your Potential Dr. Miles Monroe states "You're responsible to release your potential. No one else can, or will, do it for you. You can work hard to achieve a dream, but if you don't work hard to promote it, cultivate it, share it, and act within God's standards and directives, you will lose it". There are numerous enemies of your potential such as discouragement, procrastination, opinions of others, distractions, wrong environments, past failures, comparing yourself to others, oppositions, and many more.

The bottom line is that the devil is the ultimate enemy. Your dreams, plans, and ideas are targets of his evil forces. To stop his attacks, you must be vigilant as the Word commands. You must work out your capacity to develop, which means to work in accordance with the will of God in order to challenge and expose your potential and become relentless in your pursuit to achieve the will of God. After all, God doesn't just want us to *know* who we are in Him. He wants us to *become* who we are in Him!

1. Disobedience

Disobedience withholds the will of God. What has God told you to do that you haven't done? You will not be blessed until you do the will of God. Jonah learned the consequences of disobedience by boarding a ship going in the opposite direction from where God told him to go, and almost drowned. If God tells you to put $300 in the offering Sunday morning and you put $250, you will automatically think that you have done something great and that God will bless you. He will bless you with $250 worth of disobedience. Disobedience always wastes potential!

2. Sin

Thou shalt not . . . . The Bible is not just a book of rules designed to keep you from having fun. God knew that if we were left to our own vices, we would literally destroy ourselves. The Word of God, in essence, was given to us so we wouldn't hurt others or ourselves.

3. Fear

Fear is having faith in the impossible instead of having faith in God. In the final analysis, he who fears to try will never know what he could have done.

Four essentials of reaching your potential

1. **Diligently search your cravings.** What are you hungry for? Do you feed your flesh or your spirit?

2. **Don't ruin your appetite with junk.** Limit television and other media that appeal to your sensory perception.

3. **Exercise.** If you work out, then Jesus will work in. Don't compromise prayer; study and share your faith.

4. **Employ your gifts in a corporate setting.** Get connected to a local body of believers so you can make use of your gifts, talents, and administrations and help build the Kingdom of God.

Walking in perfection

> *And after you have suffered a little while, the God of all grace [Who imparts all blessing and favor], Who has called you to His [own] eternal glory in Christ Jesus, will Himself complete and make you what you ought to be, establish and ground you securely, and strengthen, and settle you.*

—1 Peter 5:10 (AMP)

Nothing brings out perfection like a little suffering. You may share His inheritance, but you are going to share in His suffering too!

> Therefore let us go on and get past the elementary stage in the teachings and doctrine of Christ (the Messiah), advancing steadily toward the completeness and perfection that belong to spiritual maturity. Let us not again be laying the foundation of repentance and abandonment of dead works (dead formalism) and of the faith [by which you turned] to God.[4]

To say you believe in God doesn't automatically mean you've come very far. Seeing that by now you should be much more than babes in Christ, you must get beyond the elementary principles of faith. Paul, in teaching here, gives an exhortation to press forward, which implies an active exertion to push onward to perfection, which is the mature knowledge of those who are of full age in Christian accomplishments.

Four levels of perfection

1. **Established perfection:** Where you are a dominant overcomer of sin. Sin no longer rules you.

   > Let not sin therefore rule as king in your mortal (short-lived, perishable) bodies, to make you yield to its cravings and be subject to its lusts and evil passions.[5]

2. **Cleansing perfection:** Where residual sin is cleansed out by the washing of the Word.

   > Therefore since these [great] promises are ours, beloved, let us cleanse ourselves from everything that contaminates and defiles body and spirit, and bring [our] consecration to completeness in the [reverential] fear of God.[6]

3. **Manifesting perfection:** Where your spirit has been trained by the Holy Ghost to manifest power in the physical body.

   > And wherever He came into villages or cities or the country, they would lay the sick in the marketplaces and beg Him that they might touch even the fringe of His outer garment, and as many as touched Him were restored to health.[7]

4. **Permanent perfection:** Bringing our nature into divine stability and maturity through practice.

   > Before I was afflicted I went astray, but now your word do I keep [hearing, receiving, loving, and obeying it].[8]

If you are going to reach your potential, then there is a level of spiritual maturity that must be attained. Remain accountable to perfection by adhering to God's purpose for your life, and then carrying it out at all cost!

Chapter 10

Accountability and Connectivity

As iron sharpens iron; so a man sharpens the countenance of his friend.

—Proverbs 27:17 (AMP)

Is there a man in your life who can call you out to challenge your accountability? If not, then you are playing it safe. God wants to call you out; he wants to call you out through a relationship with others. Every man of God needs a man of God, especially when it comes to speaking into each other's lives. To the degree you will allow another's influence in your life is the degree to which you will allow others to speak into your life.

It is totally awesome when men come together to connect with each other in cooperation with the Holy Spirit as we build the kingdom of God. It's rare to find this level of accountability on the job or with our families. The enemy is absolutely afraid of this. The enemy does not mind you going to church as long as your life does not impact the lives of those with whom you worship. In fact, the devil would rather you come to church and fall out with others, than for you to stay home and drink a six-pack of beer all by yourself. Why? He understands the power of unity, connectivity, and accountability.

Why is harmony so important in the church? It is important because it helps us to fulfill God's charge to reconcile the lost.

But all things are from God, Who through Jesus Christ
reconciled us to Himself [received us into favor, brought us

79

into harmony with Himself] and gave to us the ministry of
reconciliation [that by word and deed we might aim to bring
others into harmony with Him].[2]

Reconciliation is introducing the heart of man to the heart of God and
bringing those two into agreement through the power of the Holy Spirit.
"Isn't that the pastor's job?" one might ask. My reply to this is "Shepherds
beget shepherds, and sheep beget sheep!" *Go ye out* . . . is not a suggestion;
it's a demand. It's a commission—a "co-mission" between the Holy Spirit
and you in partnership.

As a young man growing up in the church, I had no real sense of
connectivity on a deeper level. The relationships I experienced during my
childhood were not very rewarding, and set the stage for events that would
take me on an emotional roller coaster throughout my earliest years and
well into my life as an adult. I would ask myself over and over again as to
how I could change my heart to keep the abandonment imposed upon me
early in life from affecting the relationships I had with other believers.

What I didn't understand at first was that "to love Christ is to care for
his body." Care equals attention, love, and encouragement. Relationships
are God's idea and are defined as the state of being related or interrelated,
connecting or binding participants, as a kinship. Relationships are the
fabric of our lives, which binds us together, making our society what it is
today. Whether we have reached the pinnacle of success or have become
disenfranchised from the mainstream of life, we simply need relationships.
The thread of that fabric unravels when we fail to realize the importance of
developing and maintaining what God had originally established for us, in
our homes, on our jobs, and in our communities. When we fail to realize
the importance that relationships have on our social infrastructures, we
become morally and ethically corrupt. We stop caring for one another, and
our lives soon become one-dimensional and self-serving.

There are many examples in the Word of God that support the idea
that relationships are of divine order. The scriptures are lucid on this point.
We should note, however, that the love of God and his desire for fellowship
with us is preeminent.

Behold, I stand at the door and knock; if anyone hears and
listens to and heeds my voice and opens the door, I will come
in to him and will eat with him, and he [will eat] with Me.[3]

It is my conviction that we are not capable of having rewarding and fulfilling relationships with each other until we learn to have a genuine, spirit-filled relationship with God. Only then can we begin to understand the various levels of relationships, which are acquaintances, working relationships, and friendship, which further relate to associations with whom we live, work, and partner. Most people rarely go beyond level two, which is working relationships. But if we are going to become effective in ministry and in reconciling the lost, it is imperative that we move beyond certain beliefs that isolate and keep us in a state of apathy toward others. Apathy and mediocrity are mind traps and comfort zones that suggest that someone else will go, someone else will help, or someone else will do it.

Moving beyond these divisive mind-sets will not happen until we begin to love God with our hearts and not just our minds. Most Christians miss God by eighteen inches, the distance between their heads and their hearts! It is only when we love God from our hearts that we truly love, care for, and connect with others on a real level. The Word of God says, "Herein do ye know that ye are my disciples, when ye have love one for another." It doesn't say when you have respect for one another or admiration. Love for one another is what God desires for us. It is through the realm of love that we move beyond the satisfaction of just being an acquaintance or having a working relationship with others.

This is where we move into the next level of relationship where we learn to give and not just take. This is also the level where we take time for others and develop friendships. God wants us to focus on developing our own character while seeking to meet the needs of those around us. The Bible says we should esteem others better than ourselves; this requires a sense of transparency as well as the aptitude to communicate with others on deeper levels. Real friends communicate with each other; this involves revealing to others how you really feel about something, such as your opinions, hopes, fears, needs, and secrets. A true friend is compatible, which means you can only be a true friend to someone with whom you're compatible.

The first place to look for compatibility is in the area of beliefs. This means that not only are you both Christians, but you both have the same convictions. Your friends will influence your belief system either for the good or for the bad. Ultimately, relationships should stir you to godliness. You should trust only those who can resist the devil, restrain the flesh, and have righteous resolve. The question you need to ask yourself is, do you want to become like the people you associate with? Real friends sacrifice and develop others. Are you willing to serve? Can you be the kind of friend who will stand by others in their lowest moments? And then, true friends forgive. We are to forgive one another as Christ has forgiven us.

From here, we begin to see the outer fringes of the next level called intimacy. The Bible says to "forsake not the assembling of ourselves together, as the manner of some is."[4] This suggests the importance of building relationships within the church. Establishing covenant with men of God in the interest of overcoming through the confession of personal sin to each other is one of the high points of accountability. It is also one of the most important aspects of Christian life as it relates to human relationship. The fact is, you will never listen to those you don't trust and never trust those you don't know.

Churches are filled with people who worship together but oftentimes do not know the name of the person they are sitting next to. It is interesting to think that someone could engage in the act of worship, which requires intimacy with God, and not become intimate with those whom we worship with.

Intimacy pertains to or is indicative of one's deepest innermost nature, characterized by informality. On this level, our lives become translucent, or like an open book. This is the level where influence is determined and the ability to receive from others, no matter how difficult the topic of discussion is. This is also the level where we open ourselves for others to read, in hopes that they too might open up enough to share life's problems.

The next level of relationship is marriage.

> And the Lord God said it is not good that the man should be
> alone; I will make him a help meet for him.[5]

This scripture has a direct correlation with the aspect of relationship in marriage. God, however, does not just want us to marry and then carry out what some consider a life sentence. His desire is that we develop a total union and oneness that allows our spouse to know everything about us and for us to know everything about them.

The Word teaches that men should love their wives as Christ loved the church and gave himself for it; and women should reverence their husbands. The reason why so many relationships and marriages become egregious is because the god of this world has blinded their minds. They are limited and held back. Even though they may be on their way to heaven, hell is controlling their lives. A renewed mind allows the Word to transform it into the image of God.

There are, however, many hindrances to this process, some of which are sociological, economical, or even generational in nature. These keep us from developing good, satisfying relationships. For instance, my abandonment as a child cut to the very essence of belief in myself and left me with the feeling that I did not want or need intimate friends. This was not because I was artificial or shallow but because I was afraid of being hurt again or left holding the bag. The possibility of rejection was more than I was willing to risk. While growing up in church, I shared many relationships with those of like faith but suffered many setbacks, and I would often sabotage many of the relationships in hopes of sparing myself from what I thought would be inevitable. There was no real evidence of change and no evidence of lasting love or joy. There were no longstanding commitments with those desiring to have and develop meaningful relationships with me.

Throughout adulthood, I continued to perpetuate wilderness experiences that kept me returning to worthless elements in my life. My receptiveness of failure came as a result of not knowing how to operate in God's spiritual system. I needed a change of heart—a change that would only come through undergoing a complete metamorphosis of the spirit, which included God's supernatural ability on top of my natural ability.

Personal transformation comes only when we understand that the mind is the control center of our lives. What we think about as well as how we perceive ourselves produces negative or positive results. Ninety percent of what goes into our minds is negative thinking—negative self-talk, negative messages, and negative things from the world.

Imagine your mind as a pool and 90 percent of what you think as the dark oily sludge of negative thoughts, which always pours in. Now imagine the positive thoughts as water that pours in at only ten percent. What happens when water and oil mix? The oily slush of pessimism always rises to the top. If you put good stuff in, then good stuff will come out. If you allow bad things to come in, then negative thinking will be in command, resulting in inappropriate behavior that will control your life. It's as simple as that! You simply have to be careful what you think.

If we are to have true change, so that we can build, repair, and maintain healthy relations, a conversion must take place in the deepest crevasses of our hearts, which allows the Word of God to transform our lives into his image so that we become renewed in the spirit of our minds. In doing so, we can develop relationships that will last a lifetime, allowing us to enter into the promises that God has set forth in his Word.

> The law of the Lord is perfect, converting the soul: the
> testimony of the Lord is sure, making wise the simple.
> The statutes of the Lord are right, rejoicing the heart: the
> commandment of the Lord is pure, enlightening the eyes. The
> fear of the Lord is clean, enduring forever: the judgments of the
> Lord are true and righteous altogether.[6]

Developing Covenant Relationships

Merriam Webster defines covenant as a formal, solemn, and binding agreement, usually under seal between two or more parties, especially for the performance of some action. Covenant relationships, as they pertain to the principles of God, are far more compelling than the views of our secular contemporaries, whose philosophies and beliefs are worldly and antithetical to his Word. The idea that one can breach a binding agreement without consequence is common in today's society. Furthermore, the lack of true covenant has greatly diminished our lives and contributed to the moral decline and ethical degeneracy of twenty-first-century civilization.

Man's relentless pursuit to eradicate the Judeo-Christian beliefs from society has left this generation without hope and in despair. Postmodern views are incongruent with the idea that the covenant was God's design, basically because of man's intent to live autonomously outside of the will of God. The breakdown of covenant relationships has even penetrated the highest office of the land where one of our country's highest executives in the White House succumbed to unsavory initiatives. His act of ill repute has galvanized negative thinking within the social order of today's culture and has unleashed a spirit of broken covenant in our land today.

The trickle-down effect has been far-reaching, especially in the inner cities of the United States where gang members display ignorance like badges of honor as they attempt to establish covenants with each other, not realizing that they greatly exacerbate their dilemmas by not embracing the greatest keeper of covenant, Christ the redeemer.

Jesus is the only one who can restore our broken lives and give us hope from our dysfunctional past. If we are to bridge gaps in our generation that divide, we must reestablish covenant relationships as a foundation, especially in the church. How we relate and interact with each other uncovers the authenticity of our faith and our love for God. Unconditional love, sacrifice, and trust are all paths that lead to establishing meaningful relations. Before Christ left his disciples, he gave them a new commandment. They were to love each other for his sake, seeking first and foremost what might benefits others, which takes sacrifice.

> Gather My godly ones to Me, those who have made a covenant
> with Me by sacrifice.[7]

Sacrifice proves the sincerity of our covenant with one another by fruits of righteousness and the surrendering of one's will. Trust, however, is the cornerstone of every covenant relationship. Salvation is a gift from God given to all who receive it, but his blessings are tied to trust.

> The heart of her husband trusts in her confidently and relies on
> and believes in her securely, so that he has no lack of [honest]
> gain or need of [dishonest] spoil.[8]

This is the description of a virtuous woman; yet it points to trust. Trust is discreet, circumspect, and considerate of every spoken word. It demonstrates to those with whom we have connection that we are governed and directed by the rules of wisdom and understanding. The law of trust is written in the heart but shows itself in the tongue. Too many relationships have been marred by what others have said. To know that one can trust another with the deepest aspects of their heart is the essence of transparency. This allows the stimulus to speak to each other on real levels.

In his book *The Power of Covenant*, Kingsley Fletcher states that covenant relationships include a built-in level of personal accountability because we relate to each other with a disarming honesty that strips away the facades and falsehoods of life. Moreover, it creates faithfulness in us individually because it births a deep desire to bring honor and joy to our covenant family. As believers, the power of the covenant must be applied to our lives daily if we are to achieve our goals to restore families, build communities, and reach a lost and dying world. We are obligated to fulfill God's will to reach mankind through the influence of covenant.

Prayer: Lord, cleanse us from secret faults and keep us from presumptuous sins. Let them not have dominion over us. Then shall we walk upright and fulfill your will to reach men through the power of covenant. Now let the words of our mouth and the meditations of our hearts be acceptable in thy sight, Oh Lord, my strength and my redeemer.

Chapter 11

Becoming His Son

But to as many as did receive and welcome Him, He gave the authority (power, privilege, right) to become the children of God, that is, to those who believe in (adhere to, trust in, and rely on) His name.

—John 1:12 (AMP)

One of the most significant and prevailing themes in society today is the ineptitudes of fathers. The fact that so many boys grow up in today's culture without the influence of their dad is shocking. Like many men, I too grew up without a relationship with my father. I think one of the worst things some men do who grow up this way is judge God by the human frailties of their fathers.

My father sired nine other children outside of his marriage with my mother. It seems, as men, we have the whole procreation thing down to a science, but when it comes to raising boys to men, regrettably we fall woefully short. Society at large has done a terrible job of teaching boys to become men, and virtually every problem we face in our culture can be traced back to this failure.

The first step in turning boys into real men is to tear down the typical criteria by which we judge each other's reputation. These include athletic ability, sexual conquest, and economic success; all of which are standards held up in society. The thought that we must excel in these areas to become successful is a lie that makes up false masculinity, eventually setting us up to fail. It gives us the concept that what we need to do as men is to compare what we have and compete with others for what we want.

For example, as a young boy I would often compare my athletic ability with others and vie for whatever attention that brought. When I got older, I compared my girlfriends with others and contended for whatever status I could acquire by being with the prettiest girl I could get. As adult males, we compare finances, houses, cars, titles, jobs, and so on. As men, this leaves us cut off from each other and destroys any real concept of community, especially in the church where we frequently walk past the very brother who in many cases is crying out for our help. It's amazing how we walk past the brokenhearted on our way to heaven. The fact is men become men in the company of men, which helps build character.

There is a difference between reputation and character. Reputation is what you and I see; character is what God sees! The church doesn't need any more talent, charisma, gifts, flamboyance, and flair. What the church needs is for men to develop character, which is a distinctive godly quality of a son of God. God is not as concerned with your talents and gifts as much as he is with your character. An example of integrity and true character is when you are all alone in the middle of the night and you're tempted to do something carnal. True godly character is being able to look that situation right in the eye and say, "I choose Jesus!" That's character!

There is a ripe harvest out there, and your laboring for it is the will of God. But in order to gather in souls, it's imperative that you live a life of purity. You must figuratively apply the blood over the doorpost of your hearts daily, sealing off every legal access to the adversary. Otherwise, you might confuse your restraint from indulging in something lascivious with deliverance.

Abstinence is not synonymous with deliverance. Just because you stop doing something for a while does not automatically mean you are delivered from it. Some men will fight the same thing for the rest of their lives while others experience total deliverance. Why is that? I'm not really sure other than the fact that some men are willing to subjugate the flesh at all cost. The litmus test of being set free is determined by what you do when you're all alone. There are times when the season of your temptation will subside. And there are times when you begin to develop higher dimensions of faith that you'll be challenged beyond what you can imagine.

Just when you decide to press into the glory is usually when that ugly thing sticks its head back up in your life. That's why you can no longer be satisfied with simply being a follower of God; you must become his son and a friend. Friendship is a polarization of interest, whereby we get beyond the point of simply using God as a handy ticket to success or an easy means of getting out of a messy situation. Jesus said, "No longer do I call you servants . . . but . . . friends." Jesus, however, made it crystal clear that friendship with him was not automatic; not all believers are his friends.

True sons of God are those who are willing to abandon their interest in exchange for his and walk in the light they have received. If a person does not follow God's Word and continues doing what he knows is wrong, then he immediately opens the door for the enemy to come in. The fact that you are required to walk in the light relates to the knowledge and illumination of God's Word that you are aware of. God is not going to hold you accountable for something you are not aware of.

But to know the will of God through his Word and to choose not to follow it brings certain defeat. Failing to do what you know to be the will of God can have a dramatic and negative impact on the results you would like to have, as well as with your sonship.

God has committed himself to bringing us into a certain place through the power of his Holy Spirit—a place of intimacy promised to the sons of God. Intimacy with Christ should be paramount and all the more important as you see the day of Christ approaching. Be the worshiper you were bought to be.

It is sad to admit, but some believers will never ascertain the deeper things of God due to their failure to renounce the carnal desires of the flesh. The flesh simply cannot and nor does it want to inhabit the realm of becoming his son, because that speaks of intimacy with Christ. The flesh seeks only itself. It seeks only to satisfy its lust thereof.

The fact is if we are to become sons of God and dwell in his presence, if we are going to enter the intimate places of his Spirit, then we must choose death. Resurrection, however, is the most important part of dying. When we die to ourselves, he will resurrect us in his presence.

> You will show me the path of life; in your presence is fullness of
> joy, at your right hand there are pleasures forevermore.[2]

If we are to truly experience what God has purposed for us and have knowledge of the pleasures that serving him holds true, then we must inhabit the secret places of the Most High.

How? By giving up our will to do his and seeking to obey him in all things and by realizing that the Spirit is given as a helper of our weaknesses and by his aid we overcome the flesh. We become sons of God when we are born again, born of water and the Spirit. We maintain our place as sons by being led by his Spirit. The Holy Spirit shows us how we must become God's children and how to continue the Christian life, which bears testimony in our lives by its fruit. Do you bear fruit of the Spirit? Does your own spirit testify that you "mind the things of the Spirit?" Does your consciousness recognize its fruit, inward as well as outward? You must be aware of your life with God, live in expectation, and walk in faith. Don't be an infant son.

One day a man went to visit a friend he hadn't seen in a few years. As they sat in the parlor, talking, the visitor noticed a young boy about the age of nine years old playing with some toys just across the hallway. He motioned for the boy to come near him. The boy responded by crawling over to where the visitor sat. The visitor suddenly realized the child was in a state of arrested development. The father, visibly saddened, dropped his head in despair.

What happened to this child? What caused this child not to grow, mentally and physically? We know from a neurological standpoint that when the bundle of nerves that sends electrical impulses to the brain becomes damaged, motor function and manual dexterity are lost. The ability to perform the simplest of task becomes nonexistent and greatly diminishes the quality of life. If this causes a person not to grow physically or mentally, I then ask, what causes us not to grow spiritually? We stop growing when we become content to visit the spirit instead of living in the spirit.

Six steps to becoming his son

1. Affirm your availability to the Lord.

> Trembling and astonished he asked, Lord, what do You desire me to do? The Lord said to him, arise and go into the city, and you will be told what you must do. [3]

God is not looking for ability; He's looking for availability. He doesn't call the qualified; He qualifies the called. You can't serve the Lord unless you serve others. "The King will answer and say to them, truly I say to you, to the extent that you did it to one of these brothers of mine, even the least of them, you did it to Me.[4]

Learning to serve is the pinnacle of what becoming a real son of God is.

2. **Assess your gifts or abilities:** "To one he gave five talents [probably about $5,000], to another two, to another one—to each in proportion to his own personal ability."[5] What God gives you must be used for him. No excuses! Your life is God's gift to you; what you do with your life is your gift to him.

3. **Accept your assignment from the Lord:** "Then Mary said, Behold, I am the handmaiden of the Lord; let it be done to me according to what you have said. And the angel left her."[6] Do whatever he says to do. Obedience is worship too!

4. **Acknowledge your accountability:** "So then every one of us shall give account of himself to God."[7] Become accountable to someone in the body. Accountability is the choice of the mature.

5. **Aim for the approval of the Lord and not of man:** "And whatsoever ye do, do it heartily, as to the Lord, and not unto men."[8] "There is no honor higher than to hear the Lord say, 'Well done, thou good and faithful servant.'"[9] This is what we should strive for.

6. **Adopt the attitude of the Lord:** "Let this same attitude and purpose and [humble] mind be in you which was in Christ Jesus: [Let Him be your example in humility:] Who, although being essentially one with God and in the form of God [possessing the fullness of the attributes which make God, God], did not think this equality with God was a thing to be eagerly grasped or retained, but stripped Himself [of all privileges and rightful dignity], so as to assume the guise of a servant (slave), in that He became like men and was born a human being."[10] The attitude of the servant should be equal with that of our Lord. Putting others first is the true attitude of a servant.

A young man was a student in a local seminary, and his professor had a profound effect on him. He felt that whenever he went to class, he was in the presence of Jesus. One day his professor died, and at the funeral, he found out why this teacher was so great. During the Great Depression era, the professor worked at the seminary not knowing when he would be paid. He also took out the church's trash and fixed tiles in the bathroom. This man was great because he was a servant. There is never a service too menial to do for the Lord!

Chapter 12

Purity

Therefore since, these [great] promises are ours, beloved, let us cleanse ourselves from everything that contaminates and defiles body and spirit, and bring [our] consecration to completeness in the [reverential] fear of God.

—2 Corinthians 7:1 (AMP)

The war over your purity is a winnable war! Your hope, however, must lie in the truth that Christ's death and resurrection defeated Satan. Now is the appointed time to learn about the power of purity and your position in Christ. Purity is defined as the quality or state of being pure and is the fuel that ignites the fires of power, authority, control, and influence in our lives through a relationship with God.

The apostle Paul said, "I appeal to you therefore, brethren, and beg of you in view of [all] the mercies of God, to make a decisive dedication of your bodies [presenting all your members and faculties] as a living sacrifice, holy (devoted, consecrated) and well pleasing to God, which is your reasonable (rational, intelligent) service and spiritual worship. Do not be conformed to this world (this age), [fashioned after and adapted to its external, superficial customs], but be transformed (changed) by the [entire] renewal of your mind [by its new ideals and its new attitude], so that you may prove [for yourselves] what is the good and acceptable and perfect will of God, even the thing which is good and acceptable and perfect [in His sight for you]."[2]

When it comes to purity, your foundation must become a rock solid understanding of who you are in Christ. We then must build upon that foundation by establishing godly relationships. Your friendships are one of the strongest guiding forces in your life, either a force for good or a force for evil. Let me stress to you that if you think that it's more important that your friends like you, rather than you please God, then you have a wrong perception of friendship. If you're influenced by your friends to do things you know are wrong, then these friendships fall into the category of evil associations. When you lie to people because you think it's what they want to hear or hang around certain individuals just to fit in with a particular group, you are playing a game that will have dire consequences on your ability to develop the power you need to become pure.

The power you seek to live pure must be preceded by your goal to become holy. God promises to empower that which he first makes holy. The Bible says that you shall receive power after the Holy Ghost is come upon you. The question is, do you want to see the power of God operate in your life? If the answer is yes, then seek to know Christ's purity of heart. Seek Jesus himself as your source.

If we are to become better husbands, fathers, and ministers of reconciliation, if we are to become real men of God, then we have to grow in holiness. A true man of God and a developed Christian will be both holy and powerful, but holiness will always precede power.

Therefore, the pureness we seek goes far beyond cleaning the outside of the cup. We are not seeking another antidote that deals with the effects but not the root cause of our human condition. We are seeking the living God. True holiness and purity do not come from following rules; they come from following Christ.

Your highest function in life is to live in the presence of God. It's where you look your best, it's where you live your best, and it's where you are your best. The ploy of the adversary is to rob us of our intimacy with God. No intimacy, no relationship! No relationship, no power!

> But you are a chosen race, a royal priesthood, a dedicated
> nation; [God's] own purchased, special people, that you may
> set forth the wonderful deeds and display the virtues and
> perfections of Him Who called you out of darkness into His
> marvelous light. Once you were not a people [at all], but now
> you are God's people; once you were un-pitied, but now you
> are pitied and have received mercy.[3]

You are a priest and a king, holy unto God so that wherever you go people may respond to him through the power that operates in your life!

You might say, "But I'm not qualified. You don't know what I've done." My response would be, "Then you don't know the power of the Holy Spirit!" God doesn't see you for who you are; he sees you for who you are becoming. It doesn't matter what you've done or whom you've done it with.

> The Lord's hand is not shortened that He cannot save;
> neither His ear heavy that it cannot hear. If we confess our
> sins He is faithful and just to forgive us and cleanse us of all
> unrighteousness.[4]

The greatest purpose of our design is for the Father to live in the inside of us. Learn to live in the Spirit instead of just visiting the Spirit every now and then.

> But now since you have been set free from sin and have become
> the slaves of God, you have your present reward in holiness and
> its end is eternal life.[5]

Build an altar of purity unto the Lord, and God will meet you there, heal you there, bless you there, and give you his name there.

Chapter 13

Finding Your Place in His Presence

Let us then fearlessly and confidently and boldly draw near to the throne of grace (the throne of God's unmerited favor to us sinners), that we may receive mercy [for our failures] and find grace to help in good time for every need [appropriate help and well-timed help, coming just when we need it].

—Hebrews 4:16 (AMP)

And the Lord said to Moses, Go and sanctify the people [set them apart for God] today and tomorrow, and let them wash their clothes and be ready by the third day, for the third day the Lord will come down upon Mount Sinai [in the cloud] in the sight of all the people.

—Exodus 19:10, 11 (AMP)

The truth is God wants to fellowship with his people. In Exodus 19, two things were to happen before the Lord came down. First, in token of cleansing themselves from sinful pollutions, the people were to wash their clothes. Not that God regards clothes, but by washing their garments, he would have them think of washing their souls by repentance. It becomes us to appear in clean clothes when we wait upon great men; so clean hearts are required in our attendance to God the Father.

Second, in demonstration of devoting themselves entirely too religious exercises, they were to abstain from lawful enjoyments during the three days and not come to their wives.

Walking into the throne room of God through the wounds of Christ is the right of every believer. Still, there are requirements to the entrance, such as repentance and contrition. God's divine wisdom was manifested to inspire the Israelites to have a profound reverence for his holiness, and nothing was more suited to this purpose than to exclude from his presence all that were polluted by any kind of uncleanness—ceremonial as well as natural, mental, and physical. God required complete purity and did not allow the children of Israel to come before him when defiled, even by involuntary or secret impurities as a want of respect due to his majesty.

When we bear in mind that God was training a people to live in his presence in some measure as priests devoted to his service, we should not regard these rules for maintenance of personal purity either too stringent or too miniscule.

> And all the people saw the thundering, and the lightning, and
> the noise of the trumpet, and the mountain smoking: and
> when the people saw it, they removed, and stood afar off. And
> they said unto Moses, Speak thou with us, and we will hear:
> but let not God speak with us, lest we die. And Moses said
> unto the people, Fear not: for God is come to prove you, and
> that his fear may be before your faces that ye sin not.[3]

They saw the lightning and heard the thunder and shrank in fear; they ran from closeness instead of pursuing him.

God loves and wants fellowship. God was calling them into his presence, but they ran the other way. We do the same thing today. Instead of making the adjustments to enter into his presence as we stop by the altar of repentance, we choose to run in the opposite direction. You might be saying, "I would have run too, considering the lightning and thundering!"

Why did God choose to show up in this manner? This was designed so they could discover the glorious majesty of God and for the assistance of their faith, that knowing the terror of the Lord they may be persuaded to live in veneration. It was also a sign of judgment in which sinners were to be called to an account for their breach of the law. Moses gave the law in such a way as to startle, affright, and humble men, that the grace and truth that came by Jesus Christ might be more welcoming. Moses encouraged them by explaining the design of God in his terror.

What they didn't understand was that the thunder and fire were not designed to consume them, which was the thing they feared. Thunder and lightning constituted one of the plagues of Egypt but were not sent to them on the same errand in which they were sent to the Egyptians.

We must not give in to consternation, the type of fear which has torment and only works for the present. Although it terrified them, it did not deter them from idolatry, for soon after this they worshiped the golden calf. This type of fear sets us trembling and engenders us to love him for the moment but soon alienates and betrays him when fleshly agendas seem more important.

We must always have in our hearts a reverence with deep respect for God's majesty, a dread of his displeasure and an obedient regard for his sovereign authority over us. This will quicken us to our duty and make us circumspect in our walking, thus standing in awe and sinning not.

Ever since Adam fled upon hearing God's voice in the garden, sinful man could not bear either to speak to God or to hear from him directly. Sin will always separate you from the fellowship of God.

> Therefore, brethren, since we have full freedom and confidence
> to enter into the [Holy of] Holies [by the power and virtue]
> in the blood of Jesus, by this fresh (new) and living way which
> He initiated and dedicated and opened for us through the
> separating curtain (veil of the Holy of Holies), that is, through
> His flesh, and since we have [such] a great and wonderful and
> noble Priest [Who rules] over the house of God, let us all come
> forward and draw near with true (honest and sincere) hearts
> in unqualified assurance and absolute conviction engendered
> by faith (by that leaning of the entire human personality on
> God in absolute trust and confidence in His power, wisdom,
> and goodness), having our hearts sprinkled and purified from a
> guilty (evil) conscience and our bodies cleansed with pure water
> so let us seize and hold fast and retain without wavering the
> hope we cherish and confess and our acknowledgment of it, for
> He Who promised is reliable (sure) and faithful to His word.[4]

It is fit that as believers we should know the honors and privileges that Christ has procured for us, such as boldness to enter into the holiest, access to him and to his light that directs us, and a right to the assurance of his acceptance. The finished work of Christ provides us with the means to enter into the gracious presence of God in his holy oracles, ordinances, providences, and covenant. It is incumbent upon us to enter into communion with him daily where we receive communications from him. It's your privilege, your God-given right, to enter into his presence. Christians enjoy such privileges by the blood of Jesus and by the merit of that blood that he offered up to God as an atoning sacrifice that he purchased for all who believe in him, granting free access to God, which gives each believer the assurance of their safety and welcomes us into his divine presence, unlike the Old Testament priests who wore bells tied to their ankles!

To the degree that you are able to find your place in his presence is the degree to which the anointing will flow through you. The anointing of the Holy Ghost is absolutely necessary for every believer. If you have accepted the Lord as your Savior, it is God's will that you be filled with his Holy Spirit.

The Bible calls us kings and priests; however, many people want to rule and dominate as a king outside his presence. If you do not take the time to minister to the Lord as priest, it will be impossible for you to rule as a king. The Bible says that those who try to obtain the power of God without being connected to him as their source are doing nothing more than performing a ritual of religiousness without true power. True power breaks the yokes and sets the captives free.

If you try to access the authority and dominion as a king and have never ministered to God as a priest, you will undoubtedly have an experience much like the seven sons of Sceva. They tried to activate the rule of the king they saw in Apostle Paul without the attentiveness to the Spirit of Christ. In other words, they liked becoming rulers and wanted the authority to cast out devils but were not authorized through the power of the Holy Ghost. They had not disposed themselves to God as priests, so therefore they had no power. I imagine their prayer went something like this: I adjure you in the name of, in the name of . . . hmm . . . What was that guy's name again? You cannot do great exploits without the power of the Holy Spirit. Understanding the many different roles of the Holy Spirit will help you have a greater appreciation for the many facets of the Spirit. In addition, it will give you deeper insights on how to tap into different realms of the anointing.

The different aspects of the Holy Spirit

Teacher

> But the Comforter (Counselor, Helper, Intercessor, Advocate, Strengthener, Standby), the Holy Spirit, Whom the Father will send in My name [in My place, to represent Me and act on My behalf], He will teach you all things. And He will cause you to recall (will remind you of, bring to your remembrance) everything I have told you."[5]

Preserver

> Now know I that the Lord will save his anointed; he will hear him from his holy heaven with the saving strength of his right hand.[6]

Keeper

> The Lord is your keeper; the Lord is your shade on your right hand [the side not carrying a shield].[7]

Yoke destroyer

> And it shall come to pass in that day, that his burden shall be taken away from off thy shoulder, and his yoke from off thy neck, and the yoke shall be destroyed because of the anointing. The anointing will disintegrate yokes so they cannot come together again.[8]

Power

> But you shall receive power (ability, efficiency, and might) when the Holy Spirit has come upon you, and you shall be My witnesses in Jerusalem and all Judea and Samaria and to the ends (the very bounds) of the earth.[9]

I remember helping a gentleman one day whose car had broken down. I was moved with compassion as the Holy Spirit urged me to lend him a hand. His car had stalled in the middle of a busy intersection and had the potential to cause a traffic accident. After we got his car to a safe place, he told me he needed a ride to the trolley station so he could get home. I agreed to take him, and off we went.

Soon after getting in my car, I noticed we didn't smell the same, and he clearly wasn't in my social economic strata. But the blood that Jesus shed at Calvary was for him too. When it comes to reconciliation and building the Kingdom of God, nothing matters more than your sensitivity to the voice of the Holy Spirit in obeying what he has told you to do even if it means rolling down your window to breathe. The bumper on my car got damaged as I pushed his car out of the road. But the damage was insignificant compared to the splendor of that man giving his heart to Jesus that day. Had it not been for the anointing of the Holy Spirit who gives us the power to witness, I would have overlooked him as everyone else had up to that point.

You have to set yourself up to be used by God. You have to become more aware of those who are in distress, both naturally and spiritually. I believe that the only time you look down on a man is when you're picking him up. The key to maximizing your effectiveness as a Christian, husband, father, and man of God is to develop a cause outside of yourself, which only occurs when you learn how to tap into the anointing. It is time for you to press into another realm of spiritual development, which is the communion of the Holy Spirit. Your heart yearns for this stage of spiritual growth.

As you become more sensitive to the Holy Spirit, you will come to know new power, new strength, new ability, and new discernment. You will learn how to walk in the Spirit, move in the power of God, know the voice of God, pray effectively, receive direction, and have the mind of Christ, which is the mind that processes the anointing, processes healing and the glory of God.

> What shall we say [to all this]? Are we to remain in sin in
> order that God's grace (favor and mercy) may multiply and
> overflow? Certainly not! How can we who died to sin live in
> it any longer? Are you ignorant of the fact that all of us who
> have been baptized into Christ Jesus were baptized into His
> death? We were buried therefore with Him by the baptism into

death, so that just as Christ was raised from the dead by the
glorious [power] of the Father, so we too might [habitually]
live and behave in newness of life. For if we have become one
with Him by sharing a death like His, we shall also be [one
with Him in sharing] His resurrection [by a new life lived
for God]. We know that our old (unrenewed) self was nailed
to the cross with Him in order that [our] body [which is the
instrument] of sin might be made ineffective and inactive for
evil, that we might no longer be the slaves of sin. For when a
man dies, he is freed (loosed, delivered) from [the power of] sin
[among men]. Now if we have died with Christ, we believe that
we shall also live with Him, because we know that Christ (the
Anointed One), being once raised from the dead, will never die
again; death no longer has power over Him. For by the death
He died, He died to sin [ending His relation to it] once for all;
and the life that He lives, He is living to God [in unbroken
fellowship with Him]. Even so consider yourselves also dead
to sin and your relation to it broken, but alive to God [living
in unbroken fellowship with Him] in Christ Jesus. Let not sin
therefore rule as king in your mortal (short-lived, perishable)
bodies, to make you yield to its cravings and be subject to its
lusts and evil passions. Do not continue offering or yielding
your bodily members [and faculties] to sin as instruments
(tools) of wickedness. But offer and yield yourselves to God as
though you have been raised from the dead to [perpetual] life,
and your bodily members [and faculties] to God, presenting
them as implements of righteousness. For sin shall not [any
longer] exert dominion over you, since now you are not under
Law [as slaves], but under grace [as subjects of God's favor
and mercy]. What then [are we to conclude]? Shall we sin
because we live not under Law but under God's favor and
mercy? Certainly not! Do you not know that if you continually
surrender yourselves to anyone to do his will, you are the slaves
of him whom you obey, whether that be to sin, which leads
to death, or to obedience which leads to righteousness (right
doing and right standing with God)? But thank God, though
you were once slaves of sin, you have become obedient with
all your heart to the standard of teaching in which you were
instructed and to which you were committed. And having been

set free from sin, you have become the servants of righteousness
(of conformity to the divine will in thought, purpose, and
action). I am speaking in familiar human terms because of your
natural limitations. For as you yielded your bodily members
[and faculties] as servants to impurity and ever increasing
lawlessness, so now yield your bodily members [and faculties]
once for all as servants to righteousness (right being and doing)
[which leads] to sanctification. For when you were slaves of
sin, you were free in regard to righteousness. But then what
benefit (return) did you get from the things of which you are
now ashamed? [None] for the end of those things is death. But
now since you have been set free from sin and have become the
slaves of God, you have your present reward in holiness and its
end is eternal life. For the wages which sin pays is death, but
the [bountiful] free gift of God is eternal life through (in union
with) Jesus Christ our Lord.[10]

The law of identification says his death, my death, his burial, my burial,
his resurrection, and my resurrection. "But the person who is united to the
Lord becomes one spirit with Him."[11] That's why Satan wants to keep
you from entering into his presence. He knows that in the Spirit, there is
singing, rejoicing, and living. He knows that when you are in the Spirit,
he can no longer drive your life. So stop giving place to something that no
longer has any power over you.

Your new confession should be thus: I am the righteousness of
God! Righteousness qualifies you to receive everything the first Adam
was supposed to have. Therefore, you are empowered to receive a
blessing—empowered to praise, empowered to worship, empowered to
live free from sin, empowered to walk upright before him, empowered to
witness, empowered to face adversity, and empowered to walk in divine
health and order. "I am crucified with Christ: nevertheless I live; yet not I,
but Christ who lives within in me: and the life which I now live in the flesh
I live by the faith of the Son of God, who loved me, and gave himself for
me."[12] This describes the spiritual or hidden life of a true believer. The old
man is crucified, but the new man is living.

And the Lord said to Moses, I will do this thing also that you
have asked, for you have found favor, loving-kindness, and
mercy in My sight and I know you personally and by name.[13]

Moses was close with God. But the term *intimacy* has lost its original meaning; many contemporaries equate intimacy almost exclusively with spousal relations. More accurately, intimacy means that I share my personal realities with you, especially my thoughts, emotions, and feelings.

Rushing off to work without acknowledging my wife makes for a bad relationship. As it is in the natural, so it is in the spiritual. We have lost the art of adoring the Lord. Familiarity with God requires a certain level of brokenness. Do you ever wonder why some people have intimacy with him while others don't? The answer is that, these are people of brokenness. The breaking of your heart arrests the eyes and ears of God that begins with a spirit of contrition and submission to his will.

The direct opposite of brokenness, however, always ends with making excuses. I would go to church but . . . . I would read my Bible but . . . . I would pray more but . . . . I would share my faith but . . . . I would go up for prayer but . . . . I would give but . . . . You just need to get your excuses out of the way.

How to enter into his presence

> *O worship the Lord in the beauty of holiness: fear before him, all the earth.*

> —Psalm 96:9 (KJV)

How you enter is determined by your hunger and thirst for him through worship. The psalmist wrote, "My soul thirsteth for the living God."[15] "Blessed are they who hunger and thirst after righteousness for they shall be filled."[16]

You may have heard the story of a Christian teacher who was training a young student in the ways of following the Lord. One day, while walking along a riverbank, the teacher asked his student to get into the water and fully submerge himself. The student was somewhat reluctant but soon obliged. The teacher suddenly held the student's head under the water until a struggle ensued. The young man forcibly overthrew his mentor and shouted, "What did you do that for?" The teacher kindly responded that the young man had to leave and could not come back until he wanted the things of God as much as he wanted to breathe.

While this illustration may seem extreme, it does point out the significance of your passion toward the things of God. In today's society, you cannot afford not to show up in his presence. Would you have the audacity not to appear in the presence of the Most High when summoned? Would you really be so callused as to keep the Creator of the universe waiting for you to respond to his call?

John, the beloved of the Lord, understood the importance of intimacy; as he lay on the Lord's chest, he heard the heartbeat of God. It was out of this relationship that God shared revelation with him and will do the same for you as you lay your head on him in total submission to his will.

Christianity is a bond, a union, not a creed or just a belief. Doing things for the church is not the same as developing a relationship with the Father. Do you ever wonder why some people after forty years of marriage get a divorce when their children are grown? They divorce because they've lost the intimacy. Just going through the motion year after year will not be enough to sustain the marriage. You must develop a closeness with each other that, in turn, will guarantee your vow of dedication.

Looking religious will not keep you in the hour of temptation. What will keep you is love for his Holy Spirit over your love for yourself. Some people have been in the church for forty years and still don't know the Father, not in the power of his resurrection, not in the fellowship of his suffering. Many people know church, but they don't know God. You can receive salvation anytime, but the blessings of God are conditional and are tied to your abiding in him.

What blocks the entrance?

Before we can enter into His presence, we must honestly and completely deal with known sin in our lives.

> But your iniquities have separated between you and your God,
> and your sins have hid his face from you, that he will not
> hear.[17]

Sometimes as believers we are startled to find out that not only are we still tempted, but also we sometimes yield to that temptation. There are two natures at work in our lives, the old sinful nature and the new spiritual nature, that wants us to live for God. Which one of these natures rules your actions? That is why it is so important to become filled with the Holy Spirit. Unless the Spirit controls our lives, we will continue to be dominated by our old nature.

The first step in being filled with his Spirit is confession of sin.

> If we say (claim) we have not sinned, we contradict His Word
> and make Him out to be false and a liar and His Word is not in
> us [the divine message of the Gospel is not in our hearts].[18]

Confession leads to repentance, which causes us to turn from sin. Some people are not sorry for what they've done, they're sorry for getting caught. Repentance leads to submission, which leads to yielding, which relates to renouncing your ways for his, placing yourself at his total disposal.

What is not the anointing

Intellectualism versus the anointing

Anyone with any degree of intellect or oratorical ability can stand on a pulpit and give a five-minute homiletic dissertation for the proliferation of the Gospel, but it's the anointing that breaks the yokes. Apostle Paul reminded the Corinthians that his speech and his preaching were not with enticing words of man's wisdom but in demonstration of the Spirit and of power. Being intellectual is fine, but let's not confuse it with the anointing.

Did you know that when you introduce foreign material to a homogeneous body, you get an exothermic reaction? Sounds deep, but what does it mean? I don't know, and I really don't care. My point is the anointing is not given to impress others. When you pray to the Father in front of other believers, you don't have to pray with a stained-glass voice. God is not impressed with your vocabulary or your ability to articulate prayer. He looks at the heart! He just wants you to be real. The glory of God will show up on every believer who knows how to receive it. But the anointing must be partaken of.

Maintaining your gifts

But clothe yourself with the Lord Jesus Christ (the Messiah), and make no provision for [indulging] the flesh [put a stop to thinking about the evil cravings of your physical nature] to [gratify its] desires (lusts).

—Romans 13:14 (AMP)

Indisputably, you'll have to give up some things to receive the anointing. There will be places you won't go, things you won't do, things you won't say, and things you won't watch or listen to in order to protect the anointing that's on your life. Whichever man (natural or spiritual) you feed, that's who is going to grow. It sounds like legalism, doesn't it? It isn't, though! Jesus paid the price, but the anointing will cost you everything. You have to exercise the spirit-man with fasting, prayer, daily Bible studies, and sharing his love with others through being committed to coming into his presence.

God is calling for people who want serious revival into a place of transparent purity; it's you he's after. He wants you to draw near. But at the same time, if you come near, he will have to deal with you. This is the same God who told Moses that no man had seen his face and lived. That can only mean one thing—you must die.

Why did Jesus wait a few extra days before coming to the place where Lazarus lay at the point of death? I'll tell you why. Because Jesus will not show up on the scene until something dies. God is calling us to a higher level of commitment. So forget your plans, lay your life down on the altar, and die to self. It's time to lay everything aside and run into his presence, realizing that nothing alive to self can stand before him. But if you die to self, he will make you alive.

Are you an eye or an ear?

It is almost embarrassing to admit that the body of Christ has become one dimensional in its pursuit to win the lost and has only one part that works, which is the mouth.

> For the body is not one member, but many." If the foot shall
> say, because I am not the hand, I am not of the body; is it
> therefore not of the body? And if the ear shall say, because I
> am not the eye, I am not of the body; is it therefore not of the
> body? If the whole body were an eye, where was the hearing? If
> the whole were hearing, where is the smelling? But now hath
> God set the members every one of them in the body, as it hath
> pleased him.[20]

Two lumberjacks were felling trees one day in different camps. One lumberjack noticed the other guy was cutting down twice as many trees as he was and decided to go over to the other camp to see why. When he got there, he noticed that his friend was not using an axe but had some newfangled device with a saw blade driven by a chain attached to a motor. He was completely amazed at his friend's production and asked if he could try out this new piece of equipment for the rest of the day. His friend agreed, and off he went. An hour later, he brought it back and said, "I can't use this thing. Here—take it!"

His friend asked, "Why? What is wrong with it?"

The man snapped, "It doesn't chop right!"

I'll give you a few seconds to collect yourself . . . one, one thousand, two, one thousand. Okay. What's the moral? The moral is that you should use what God has given you and stop wasting time trying to be someone or something you are not. Don't let your lofty ideas get you into places where you are not anointed to stand. I know plenty of pastors who should be evangelists and plenty of evangelists who should be pastors. The bottom line is your gifts will make room for you. Just be ready and stay prepared. Opportunity usually shows up with overalls on and requires real work.

Don't ever sidestep a chance to work with other men at your church! Especially when you know there won't be any recognition for the work you will do! This not only helps you to connect with other men on deeper levels, but it builds character too. Your commitment to what you are asked to do is crucial to your growth. Being devoted means you can be counted on and not just counted. Your pastor doesn't just want to count you as a number in the crowd; he wants to know you're part of the assembled crowd and that he's able to count on your service to the church. If you're truly committed, you can be counted on at any time. Faithfulness is not defined by your attendance but by your service.

Have you been faithful to the ministry God has given you? Most would have to say no! If you were asked to explain what your personal ministry is, 95 percent could not do it. How can you be faithful to something when you don't know what it is? As you read this book, you are participating in my ministry. My assignment is to equip you to discover what God wants you to do, by walking down the path of purity so that you will have the power to do it. Your assignment is to find the will of God for your life and then get behind that with all your heart.

A man wanted to become a missionary to China and consulted with his pastor.

"Do you speak Chinese?" the pastor asked.

"No," he replied.

"Do you have the finances to go?"

"No!"

"Do you have obligations here?"

"Yes."

"Then you are better off here," said the pastor. "By the time you learn Chinese, you will be at the end of your life. Stay here and send support to those who are there." That was good advice.

When you decide God is speaking to you about your calling, make sure it's his voice and not yours. When making decisions, you should have the peace of God in your heart. When that peace is disturbed, stop! The difference between his perfect will and his permissive will is that his perfect will is what he intended and his permissive will is what he allows.

Sometimes you need to investigate your motives closer so you can stop making wrong choices and really hear what God is saying to you. Just know that provision will always show up at the point of your assignment. And your assignment usually has something to do with problems others are facing that you have the God-given wisdom to solve. In other words, things that sadden you like children going hungry, which could be the indication of an assignment for you to help heal others. When you take hold of your legacy by helping others in need, God will supply. Supply what? Whatever you need to accomplish his will.

Spiritual gifts

The Holy Spirit, for the purpose of building up the church, bestows spiritual gifts upon Christians. They include wisdom, knowledge, faith, healing miracles, prophecy, discerning of spirits, speaking in tongues, and interpretation of tongues. Since these gifts are gifts of grace, according to Apostle Paul, their use must be controlled by the principle of love—the greatest of all spiritual gifts. The following is a list that describes certain characteristics of several gifts and administrations already mentioned.

Preaching: This is a verbal declaration of the truth. The preacher is known as the eyes of God; he is a gifted member who desires, confirms, and reinforces God's standards and truths to others.

Prophesying: The prophet often says, "Let's pray about it." He carries a "John the Baptist" mantle (repent and be born again).

Helping: The server meets the practical needs in the church; (muscle, helper) renders service, aid, and the relief of others.

Teaching: It clarifies and explains the truth. The teacher helps instill the truth into others and instructs others to support the church. He teaches whether you like it or not; studies and reads all the time; has books on top of books. Information and detail oriented. Likes to make lists, giving detailed information and explaining how things should work.

Exhorting: The encourager says, "Let me show you." An exhorter is a spiritual cheerleader who sees potential in every situation that comforts, consoles, encourages, and strengthens others on a personal level. He has faith for everyone and stays excited. He encourages others to hang in there and not give up.

Giving: The giver invests heavily in the work of God. He is one who helps to meet the financial needs and stimulates others to give on a personal basis. He is gifted to give without an outward show. He operates under the principles of seedtime and harvest. He is convinced gifts will produce spiritual results. He will give even when it is not God's will.

Ruling: The ruler is organizational and administrative (thinker or doer). He is one who leads by good example and faithful service. He helps to organize, set, and meet the goals of the ministry. He cannot stand chaos and disorder, likes details, and will take over a project if you are too slow. He is mostly misunderstood, and he often has uptight status but gets things done.

Having mercy: The one who has mercy is a feeler, one who is motivated to encourage, love, and show compassion with sincere motives. He says, "I understand. Let's cry together."

Three principles to help you discover your ministry

(1) Find out what gets you excited.
(2) Find out what you're naturally good at.
(3) Determine how the things you are naturally good at impact others.

If it doesn't impact others to God's glory, then you need to keep discovering. Discover and implement your gifts in cooperation with God; otherwise you may miss your purpose in life.

Chapter 14

A New Beginning

Therefore if any person is [engrafted] in Christ (the Messiah) he is a new creation (a new creature altogether); the old [previous moral and spiritual condition] has passed away. Behold the fresh and new have come!

—2 Corinthians 5:17 (AMP)

Paul taught that the spiritual mind is life and peace. This means that until the seat of our consciousness—which generates thoughts, feelings, ideas, and perceptions—is renewed, we will still be conformed to this world. If you try to change your attitudes or behaviors without dealing with your basic mind-set, the changes will only be temporary. Soon your mind will lead you back to the same problems all over again. If you are going to change your life, then you have to change your mind.

Becoming a new creature means to follow God's pathway. You can't be led and driven at the same time. If your flesh is in control, then you are driven. When we receive Jesus Christ into our lives, he then controls our lives, making all the promises of God available to us. We experience these promises in our lives when we live as God directs. This means to walk in his Spirit and in the truth, which always results in fulfillment, satisfaction, and peace.

For He satisfies the longing soul, and fills the hungry soul with goodness.[2]

How would you like to start over? How would you like a clean slate? What would you do differently if you could? Do you need a new beginning? Before we talk about new beginnings, let's first talk about conformity. *Conformed* means to be shaped from the outside in; *transformed* means to be shaped from the inside out. You need to be conformed to the Word of God, not the world's system. Whatever is your age, that's how long you have been influenced by the world's system. The reformation you seek comes from complying with the Word of God. Someone coined the phrase "a mind is a terrible thing to waste." Well, so are the promises of God. Unless you replace the things that are no longer suitable for your spiritual progression, you are not capable of receiving the untold riches of God.

First of all, you don't realize they exist. Second, you don't recognize they belong to you. Have you ever noticed people who look for money on the ground? A lot of their time is spent simply looking for things others have dropped. I'm not trying to condemn this practice, but I would point out that all good and perfect gifts come from above, both physically and spiritually.

You don't have to adopt a beggar's mentality as your mind might suggest. The unchanged mind will have you accept things the way they are because your parents did. Just because your dad was an alcoholic, it doesn't mean you are going to be one. It is important that you reshape your thinking about yourself. You cannot afford to waste any more time by doing things the same old way. If you want to keep getting what you're getting, then keep doing what you are doing.

Most of us have the right address, the right cars, and the right economic status. We seemingly have arrived! But when you pray, do you have the assurance that God the Father will answer your prayers? When someone asks your advice about a tough situation, is your response based on the Word of God or your own philosophy? Do you know the promises of God as stated in his Word?

A young man, whose dad was very wealthy, was graduating from high school and was about to enter his first year of college. He asked his father for a brand-new car as a graduation present. His father told him he would look into the matter. On graduation day, the father presented his son with a brand-new Bible instead and told him to read it daily because it contained untold treasures. The boy was obviously disappointed but thanked his dad and tried not to show his dissatisfaction.

After a year away at school, the young man began to miss home and became depressed after being put on academic probation. He remembered his father telling him to read his Bible often, especially when things weren't going well. He hadn't read it that whole year but decided it would probably be a good time to start. He took the Bible down off the shelf and began to read it. He found an envelope inside and opened it. To his surprise, he found the pink-slip to the new car he had asked his father for a year earlier. Apparently, his father had made arrangements with the automobile dealer to keep the car that was paid for until his son claimed it.

The irony is, like the young man in this story, many today neglect receiving their blessings because they fail to claim what is rightfully theirs through the knowledge of his Word. All the young man had to do was claim it. It was paid for! What has the blood of Christ paid for that you haven't claimed?

Many will not receive what belongs to them solely because they do not spend time in the Word. Unless you spend quality time in the Word of God, you are not capable of having a new beginning simply because the mind cannot change unless it is regenerated by the Word of God. Your perception to things in life will stay the same. You will remain reactive rather than proactive, negative rather than positive, pessimistic instead of optimistic. The Word gives us an exhortation to "put off concerning the former conversation the old man, which is corrupt according to the deceitful lusts; and be renewed in the spirit of your mind."[3]

What does the Bible have to say about new beginnings?

> Brethren, I count not myself to have apprehended: but this
> one thing I do, forgetting those things which are behind, and
> reaching forth unto those things which are before.[4]

New beginnings begin where remembering your past ends. Whether it's past sins, misfortunes, or setbacks, you simply must forget it and move on. Paul forgot the things that were behind so as not to be content with past grace or labors or present measures of grace. He reached forth and stretched himself toward his point; this expression shows great concern to be more and more like Christ.

He who runs a race must never stop short of the end but press forward as fast as he can. So those who have heaven in their view must still press forward to it in holy desires, hopes, and constant endeavors. You cannot lean back on your laurels of accomplishment. Do not think for one moment that you can afford to rest, because there are always higher heights and deeper depths. Nothing would please the devil more than for you to take ease and accept the placebo that he offers you, which is to do nothing more at your church than just show up.

God's way versus the world's

God's way says do unto others as you would have others do unto you. The world says to do them in before they do you in.

God's way says, "Give and it shall be given unto you." The world asks, "What's in it for me?"

The old nature

The old nature does not care about God or the things of God. It does not care to pray, fast, or tell anyone about the goodness of the Lord. The old nature is continually sinful and has a disdain for spiritual things.

> For I know that in me (that is, in my flesh,) dwelleth no good thing: for to will is present with me; but how to perform that which is good I find not.[5]

The old nature is corrupt!

> For from within, out of the heart of men, proceed evil thoughts, adulteries, fornications, murders, thefts, covetousness, wickedness, deceit, lasciviousness, an evil eye, blasphemy, pride, foolishness. All these evil things come from within, and defile the man.

The old nature seeks to please itself and loves the things of the world—the lust of the flesh, the lust of the eye, and the pride of life! In fact, if allowed, the old man will totally resurrect himself. All you have to do is feed him. Our wills are trained to our flesh. It took some of you many years to get the way you are. Now you have to train your will to your spirit. If someone makes you mad and you agree with your flesh, which says you're offended, then your agreement is wrong. Instead, you need to agree with your spirit, which says to pray for those who mistreat or despitefully use you. Just know that dead men don't get offended, affronted, insulted, hurt, slighted, or snubbed. And if you are easily offended, then you haven't died to some things yet and need healing in that area of your heart.

When you feel nervous or anxious about something, the flesh says, "It's time for a drink."

The Spirit says, "Cast your care upon me."

When you can't seem to relax, the old nature says, "You need to smoke."

The Spirit says, "Rest in my rest!"

When you feel lonely, the flesh says, "Call that loose girl."

The Spirit says, "Abide in me. I will never leave you."

Every choice or decision we make must lead to God. Don't let your flesh make decisions. As men of God, we must make wise choices that lead our families and others in the direction of God. Spirit-filled choices depend on your devotion, consecration, sanctification, and intimacy with God. You must develop a lifestyle of fasting and prayer. You need to know he is a keeper if you want to be kept. Should you make a mistake, it's not over; repent, get up, and try it again. The Lord will never give up on you. You are free from condemnation and guilt.

> If the Son therefore shall make you free, ye shall be free
> indeed.[7]

Yet that freedom comes with great responsibility. You still need to be accountable to the Lord, especially when temptation strikes. The fact is you are going to have to suffer through the flesh.

> Forasmuch then as Christ hath suffered for us in the flesh,
> arm yourselves likewise with the same mind: for he that hath
> suffered in the flesh hath ceased from sin; that he no longer
> should live the rest of his time in the flesh to the lusts of men,
> but to the will of God.[8]

Keep in mind that the old nature cannot endure affliction, heartache, pain, or adversity. It's going to take becoming a new creature to get you through. Only a direct encounter with God can prepare you to face the challenges ahead.

How to become a new creature

Confess: To confess means to agree with God.

> I acknowledged my sin to You, and my iniquity I did not hide.
> I said, I will confess my transgressions to the Lord [continually
> unfolding the past till all is told]—then You [instantly] forgave
> me the guilt and iniquity of my sin. Selah.[9]

Forsake sin.

> He that covereth his sins shall not prosper: but whoso confesses
> and forsakes them shall have mercy.[10]

Accept God's forgiveness.

> For by grace are ye saved through faith; and that not of
> yourselves: it is the gift of God: not of works, lest any man
> should boast.[11]

In order to become a new creation, you must have a road-to-Damascus experience. This is an undeniable involvement with the Lord that will bring you to the end of yourself, forever changing your life, to the point that, eventually, the similarities and attributes of the Father become evident. After years of relationship, my son should resemble me in some way. A guy complained to a judge about having to pay child support for someone he didn't think was his son. The man spitefully told the judge, "He doesn't even look like me!" The judge told the man to keep feeding the lad and he would start to look like him after a while. You must eat the Word of God daily if you are going to look like your heavenly Father. After all, we grow to resemble that which we love.

Steps in maintaining your walk with Christ

Practice submission and surrender.

> Submit therefore to God.[12]

Have a set mind.

> Thou wilt keep him in perfect peace, whose mind is stayed on thee, because he trusteth in thee.[13]

Take the chosen path.

> Make me to go in the path of thy commandments; for therein do I delight.[14]

Walk the daily walk.

> Therefore thou shalt keep the commandments of the Lord thy God, to walk in his ways, and to fear him.[15]

Set right priorities.

> Set your affection on things above, not on things on the earth.[16]

Learn to talk differently.

> Death and life are in the power of the tongue, and they that love it shall eat the fruit thereof.[17]

Sing a new song.

> And he hath put a new song in my mouth, even praise unto our God: many shall see it, and fear, and shall trust in the Lord.[18]

When Jesus is the center of our lives, he teaches us how to think in the Spirit and provides the direction and strength we need to maintain balance, which leads to a transformed life. Walk in righteousness and true holiness. Learn to dwell in the Word through reverence and knowing how to respond to it. Protect, keep, and defend God's Word. Allow it to be the standard by which you live. Remember that your past cannot keep you from entering into the future that God has planned for you, unless you let it.

Never again will I confess I can't.

I have strength for all things in Christ who empowers me [I am
ready for anything and equal to anything through Him who
infuses inner strength into me; I am self-sufficient in Christ's
sufficiency].[19]

Never again will I confess lack.

And my god will liberally supply (fill to the full) your every
need according to His riches in glory in Christ Jesus.[20]

Never again will I confess fear.

For God did not give us a spirit of timidity (of cowardice, of
craven and cringing and fawning fear), but [He has given us
a spirit] of power and of love and of a calm and well-balanced
mind and discipline and self-control.[21]

Never again will I profess weakness.

The Lord is my Light and my Salvation—whom shall I fear or
dread? The Lord is the Refuge and Stronghold of my life—of
whom shall I be afraid?[22]

Never will I confess the supremacy of Satan over my life or live in
peaceful coexistence with him.

Little children, you are of God [you belong to Him] and
have [already] defeated and overcome them [the agents of the
antichrist], because He Who lives in you is greater (mightier)
than he who is in the world.[23]

Never again will I confess defeat.

But thanks be to God, Who in Christ always leads us in
triumph [as trophies of Christ's victory] and through us spreads
and makes evident the fragrance of the knowledge of God
everywhere.[24]

Never again will I confess lack of wisdom.

> But it is from Him that you have your life in Christ Jesus,
> Whom God made our Wisdom from God, [revealed to us a
> knowledge of the divine plan of salvation previously hidden,
> manifesting itself as] our Righteousness [thus making us
> upright and putting us in right standing with God], and our
> Consecration [making us pure and holy], and our Redemption
> [providing our ransom from eternal penalty for sin].[25]

Never again will I profess sickness.

> He personally bore our sins in His [own] body on the tree [as
> on an altar and offered Himself on it], that we might die (cease
> to exist) to sin and live to righteousness. By His wounds you
> have been healed.[26]

Never again will I profess worries or frustration.

> Casting the whole of your care [all your anxieties, all your
> worries, all your concerns, once and for all] on Him, for He
> cares for you affectionately and cares about you watchfully.[27]

Never again will I profess bondage.

> Now the Lord is the Spirit, and where the Spirit of the Lord is,
> there is liberty (emancipation from bondage).[2]

Chapter 15

Healing Your Marriage

So He said to them, you will doubtless quote to Me this proverb:
Physician, heal yourself! What we have learned by hearsay that you
did in Capernaum, do here also in your [own] town.

—Luke 4:23 (AMP)

The power to heal your marriage is in your hands. Satan knows that his time is short! One of his last acts of defiance is to try and destroy families. Satan, who separated a third of the angels in heaven, still uses this age-old tactic to separate families today. Division and separation are demonic, and the strategy behind them is to divide and conquer.

The answers to your marital problems and to the healing of your marriage lie in the truth that someone must sacrifice. The question is, do you love God passionately enough to be the one who chooses death? It should not be a question of "Why do I have to?" Instead, it should be stated, "I'm glad I get to," realizing that sacrifice and reconciliation delight the Father. When you make up your mind to reconcile, it delivers a mighty blow to the devil. Satan is not bound by the one who can yell, "Get thee behind me!" the loudest but by the one who decides to live through death. If your marriage is going to become healthy again, then you must die to your flesh. If you are unhappy, depressed, and miserable in your marriage, then your flesh is alive, well, and ruling every situation you face.

Jesus said, "If any man come after me, let him deny himself take up his cross and follow me."[2] The key is to take up the Cross. The Cross, however, is not that which you do not choose, that is, loss of a job, sickness, and so on. The Cross is that which you willfully choose, that which makes your flesh agonize. Jesus said, "If there is any other way." How do you know when you've really died? You know when that person pokes you again and you don't react or defend. Instead, out pours blood and water, redemption and refreshment, not vinegar.

Jesus died shockingly early; they couldn't believe how quickly he went. He knew the sooner he died, the quicker the resurrection. Your resurrection will come sooner when you choose to die to your flesh quicker. You must choose the cup. Do you love the Lord at all? Do you love Jesus enough to die? If so, then leave your gift at the altar, and go and get your relationship altered.

In addition to that, add five words to your vocabulary that can divorce-proof your marriage. *There is no way out!* You don't need to write it down; it's already in your heart.

Men, God is expecting you to follow through with your wives. Your success as a husband is equal to your ability to love, nurture, and help bring your wife's dreams to fruition. Don't you dare think for one moment that you can treat her any way you like and still reach optimum levels of achievement and success.

Here are twelve more words that I suggest you write down and commit to memory, so the next time you have an intense moment of fellowship with your wife, you can help the situation by saying these words. They are as follows: *I am sorry. I was wrong. Please forgive me. I love you.*

In many cases, however, just saying "I'm sorry" will have little or no effect. Why? Because at best, this forces two people to behave a certain way without resolving the deeper inner conflicts that separate their lives. Marriage will always bring out what's already there. What am I saying? I'm saying you have to get to the root cause of your problems. You have to get rid of the baggage that separates you.

Two things you must do to start the healing process

(1) **Make God a priority in your lives.** Put him first, your mate second, and yourself last!

(2) **Be committed to each other.** Marriage is not a feeling; it's a commitment. The secret of a long marriage is that of devotion. You should marry for commitment, and not just love, because

commitment runs north and south, while love runs east and west, depending on how you are acting. Eventually, love will ebb and flow with the vicissitudes of life. Just stay with it. Commitment is not a contract; it is an act of the will. A contract says, "I can get out if it doesn't work." Commitment says, "I am yours for life, and no matter what happens, I am willing to work out the problem whatever it may be." Good and bad marriages face the same problems; the difference is that of commitment.

Communication

That the communication of thy faith may become effectual by the acknowledging of every good thing which is in you in Christ Jesus.

—Philemon 1:6 (KJV)

Statistically, 50 percent of divorces report communication problems. Contrary to popular belief, the appendages stuck to the side of your head are there for other reasons than just holding up your sunglasses. The fact that God gave you two ears and one mouth is indicative of his wanting you to listen twice as much as you speak.

A woman went to a marriage counselor frantic that her husband was going to leave her. The counselor asked what the problem was, and the woman responded by saying, "My husband always complains about not being able to communicate with me."

The counselor then asked the woman, "Does he have a grudge?"

The woman replied, "Why, no, he doesn't have a grudge. He has a carport." Okay, moving right along.

You are going to make mistakes; you are going to annoy each other sometimes. Therefore, you need some practical means of solving your differences, which should start with you learning to communicate better. My wife and I use the pen method. When she speaks, she holds the pen, and when she finishes speaking, making her point she passes the pen to me so that I can respond. If you develop better means of communicating, your relationship will be more secure. Did you know that the health of your marriage is determined by how quickly you can agree after an argument? Try holding hands while talking, as this will help keep a lid on the situation when things get out of control.

Why do you think it is said "things got out of hand?" The sense of touch has an effect like no other sensory perception. The sense of touch has been said to even lower high blood pressure. Just the caring touch of someone's hand can bring calm to any situation that may arise.

Don't tear one another down with words

> Let no foul or polluting language, nor evil word, nor unwholesome or worthless talk ever come out of your mouth, but only such speech as is good and beneficial to the spiritual progress of others, as is fitting to the need and of the occasion, that it may be a blessing and give grace (God's unmerited favor) to those who hear it!

—Ephesians 4:29 (AMP)

> But I say unto you, that every idle word that men shall speak, they shall give account thereof in the Day of Judgment.

—Matthew 12:36 (KJV)

Idle words mentioned here are powerless words that produce no good effects. These are words that cut instead of make whole—like sarcasm, which is the tool of the weak. If you constantly tear down your spouse with remarks that mean the opposite of what they seem to say, words that are intended to mock or deride, the Bible says that you will give account to.

There is simply no problem you cannot solve if you are both willing to communicate. It is not an option; it is an essential element. You need to talk about everything. So speak the truth in love, build each other up, and encourage each other! When all else fails, just say something like, "My love for you burns with the white hot intensity of a thousand suns." And then stand back and watch her melt.

Designed for desire: Sex

Adam: God, what are those animals doing?
God: What?
Adam: You know!

God: What?
Adam: You know that!

> And the Lord God said it is not good that the man should be
> alone; I will make him a help meet for him.[6]

When Adam awoke out of sleep, the Lord said, "Well, what are you going to call her?"

Adam took one look at Eve and said, "Whoa! Man!"

There is no greater measure of love than when married couples express their affection for each other through the union of sexual intimacy. There will be nights when you know she is just doing her duty to love you, and there will be other nights you'll think she's intoxicated with love. There will be plenty of nights when you know she is just acting out of obedience, and then there will be other nights when she'll say, "Honey, I just don't feel like it tonight." And you'll say, "That's quite all right, dear," and you'll go to sleep. You need to express nonsexual intimacy with your wife from time to time. It's called romance. Simply put, your wife needs to know that you enjoy being with her without any strings attached and that you would rather spend time with her than anyone else.

Nurturing and involvement take care of her emotional needs. Praying and studying with your wife provide her the stability and strength of knowing you are the spiritual head and leader of the home. She wants to know you see great value in her, not just when you feel romantic. She needs to feel understood and protected. Your wife is the garden of your soul, and you are the seed of the trees of that garden.

Note the wedding ring and its round contour. It is the quintessential example of something that has no beginning or ending, which signifies unity between two people. I don't know when my love for my wife began, and I certainly don't see its end. Allow your wife to become an expression of your love as the two of you become one!

When forgiveness seems impossible

> *Take heed to yourselves: If thy brother trespass against thee, rebuke him; and if he repent, forgive him.*

—Luke 17:3 (KJV)

Forgiveness and reconciliation are two different things. Reconciliation relates to the restoration of the relationship. To do this you must have agreement on both sides. Forgiveness, on the other hand, is the release or pardon to the point that when you look at them you are no longer embittered. The power to forgive is found in the acknowledgment of your own forgiveness. Not forgiving someone is like you drinking poison and expecting the other person to die. It will eventually kill you.

A young lady once asked me what she should do about her husband who had committed adultery and had given her a sexually transmitted disease. My first question to her was "Do you love him?" My second question was "Do you want your marriage to be healed?" To both, she replied yes. I told her that with God all things were possible and that he could heal her.

Don't misunderstand me. I wasn't oversimplifying the matter by undermining her pain. This woman was deeply hurt. It may take years for her to completely heal and begin to trust her husband again. It would now be the burden of the man to rebuild the broken trust. Her job would be to allow the Holy Ghost to mend her broken heart.

As Christians, God did not make us rugs for people to walk on. He told us to be wise as serpents but gentle as doves. I told her in no uncertain terms that if she decided to try to make things work, she would have to make sure he understood this was a one-time deal and that she was not going to accept it if it ever happened again. I further stated that if he were truly sorry, then he would change. This is a very extreme circumstance that will take time to heal, as the power of God washes the marriage, making it a model of his grace and ability to reconcile even the most hopeless of situations.

Forgiveness is tied to your future

> Truly I tell you, whoever says to this mountain, be lifted up and thrown into the sea! And does not doubt at all in his heart but believes that what he says will take place; it will be done for him. For this reason I am telling you, whatever you ask for in prayer, believe (trust and be confident) that it is granted to you, and you will [get it]. And whenever you stand praying, if you have anything against anyone, forgive him and let it drop (leave it, let it go), in order that your Father Who is in heaven may also forgive you your [own] failings and shortcomings and let them drop. But if you do

not forgive, neither will your Father in heaven forgive your failings and shortcomings. For verily I say unto you, That whosoever shall say unto this mountain, Be thou removed, and be thou cast into the sea, and shall not doubt in his heart, but shall believe that those things which he saith shall come to pass; he shall have whatsoever he saith. Therefore I say unto you, what things so ever ye desire, when ye pray, believe that ye receive [them], and ye shall have them. And when ye stand praying, forgive, if ye have ought against any: that your Father also which is in heaven may forgive you your trespasses. But if ye do not forgive, neither will your Father which is in heaven forgive your trespasses.

—Mark 11:23-26 (KJV)

Forgiveness costs but ultimately pays. You cost Jesus his life, and it will cost you as well. It will cost you your pride, vanity, egotism, and self-centeredness. You have to humble yourself. This is not a battle between you and her. It is a battle for your children's future. You might be thinking, *But I just don't love her anymore!* My response to that is "Ask God to give you the love you need to stay in that relationship. And then make-believe that love is already there." In other words, "Do the things you once did for her until love catches up."

On the other hand, if you no longer love her because you are in a relationship with someone else, then you are dead in your trespasses and sins. How can you make a dead man see or feel? How can you convince a man in this condition that he needs to change? You can't. It's impossible! Dead men don't respond because dead men don't feel anything. They especially don't feel the conviction of sin.

I thank God for the Holy Spirit who brings us to the place of undeniable conviction where we hear the Lord say, "Awake thou that sleepeth, arise from the dead, and I will give thee life."

There is no greater miracle than for those who were lost in the trespasses of their sins to see the light of the Gospel and receive the Lord Jesus into their hearts. The difficult task rests with the wives of such men in allowing the Holy Ghost to do what he does best, and that is to draw men to Jesus.

Suggestions for marriages in trouble

(1) Don't consider divorce.
(2) Don't compare your mate or marriage to others.
(3) Stop all criticism. Love doesn't criticize or find fault.
(4) Start talking. Men, ask her what your biggest fault is; ask her to help you.
(5) Cease any relationship outside of the marriage where affection is sought.
(6) Trust your mate.
(7) Do something every day to please your mate.

> Finally, all [of you] should be of one and the same mind
> (united in spirit), sympathizing [with one another], loving
> [each other] as brethren [of one household], compassionate and
> courteous (tenderhearted and humble). Never return evil for
> evil or insult for insult (scolding, tongue-lashing, berating), but
> on the contrary blessing [praying for their welfare, happiness,
> and protection, and truly pitying and loving them]. Know that
> to this you have been called, that you may yourselves inherit a
> blessing [from God—that you may obtain a blessing as heirs,
> bringing welfare and happiness and protection]. For let him
> who wants to enjoy life and see good days [good—whether
> apparent or not] keep his tongue free from evil and his
> lips from guile (treachery, deceit). Let him turn away from
> wickedness and shun it, and let him do right. Let him search
> for peace (harmony; and peace from fears, agitating passions,
> and moral conflicts) and seek it eagerly. [Do not merely desire
> peaceful relations with God, with your fellowmen, and with
> yourself, but pursue, go after them!] For the eyes of the Lord
> are upon the righteous (those who are upright and in right
> standing with God), and His ears are attentive to their prayer.
> But the face of the Lord is against those who practice evil [to
> oppose them, to frustrate, and defeat them].[9]

Afterword

Become a giver. Why? Giving unconditionally from your heart allows you to tap into the reciprocities of God—not just from a financial standpoint but from the aspect of receiving everything that you need from him so that you can be a blessing to others, which is the highest order of being a Christian! Whether it's health, a better marriage relationship, or deliverance from an addiction, giving opens the windows of heaven for you to receive. Mount Hermon is a snow-capped mountain just west of Damascus. Its elevation is about 9,232 feet above sea level. The Jordan River, which runs near the slopes of Mount Hermon, flows through the Sea of Galilee and finally drains into the Dead Sea.

The Sea of Galilee is 686 feet below sea level and enjoys a pleasant climate. The landmass surrounding this lake is very fertile and bustles with fruitfulness.

The Dead Sea has a desolate forbidding landscape surrounding the sea. It's the lowest body of water on the earth at 1,312 feet below sea level. Because of its high salt content nothing lives in or around the sea. It's called the Dead Sea because of its stagnant condition. Sodom and Gomorrah lie submerged beneath the southern end of the Dead Sea.

The difference between these two bodies of water—the Sea of Galilee and the Dead Sea—is that one receives and gives; the other receives and keeps.

> For God so greatly loved and dearly prized the world that
> He [even] gave up His only begotten (unique) Son, so that
> whoever believes in (trusts in, clings to, relies on) Him shall
> not perish (come to destruction, be lost) but have eternal
> (everlasting) life.[10]

When you fall in love with Christ, you become a giver. You can give without loving, but you can't love without giving. Don't become like this great body of water that has great potential but has become stagnant because of its inability to give. When you give out of your heart, you show the Lord your trust. You show the Lord your confidence that he will perform his Word. The Bible says to "give and it shall be given unto you, good measure shaken together, running over, shall men give into your bosom."[11]

You are blessed and empowered to succeed, anointed to prosper, and impossible to curse. You are the instrument of his favor. So remember to praise until worship comes, worship until the glory comes, and then stand in the glory. God cannot lie; he will not fail, and he will not deny his own.

If you are going to take the road that leads to purity, then you must always walk down the center of that road. To venture along the outer edge is to invite peril and possibly jeopardize the sobriety, which you've worked so hard to achieve. Walking along the outer fringes of that purity and taking glimpses of unsavory things in life is a recipe for disaster. Walking along the perimeters of life causes one to chance falling into the many trenches and pitfalls along the sides. Keep to the center of the road by developing a passion to be pure, which will always create the need to make required changes when they become necessary. Stay pure and receive God's richest blessings!

Endnotes

Chapter 1: Every Man's Fight

1. See 1 Timothy 6:12 (AMP)
2. See Romans 8:13 (AMP)

Chapter 2: Thirty-Three Years of Bondage

1. See Exodus 6:6 (AMP)
2. See John 5:1-9 (AMP)

Chapter 3: Why You Must Win This Battle

1. See Romans 8:19 (AMP)

Chapter 4: Warfare

1. See 1 Timothy 1:18 (AMP)
2. See 1 Samuel 17:38, 39 (AMP)
3. See Luke 11:21, 22 (AMP)
4. See 1 Peter 5:8 (AMP)
5. See 2 Corinthians 10:4 (AMP)
6. See Ephesians 6:10-18 (AMP)
7. See Romans 13:11, 12 (AMP)
8. See John 3:21 (AMP)
9. See Isaiah 59:17 (AMP)

10. See Ephesians 6:15 (AMP)
11. See Ephesians 6:16 (AMP)
12. See Ephesians 6:17 (AMP)
13. See 1 Thessalonians 5:4-8 (AMP)
14. See Romans 13:13, 14 (AMP)
15. See Ephesians 6:17 (AMP)
16. See Hebrews 4:12 (AMP)
17. See Ephesians 6:18 (AMP)

Chapter 5: Resisting the Enemy

1. See James 4:7 (AMP)
2. See James 4:8-10 (AMP)
3. See Romans 6:11 (AMP)

Chapter 6: Overcoming Temptation

1. See James 1:13-15 (AMP)
2. See Genesis 3:5-6 (AMP)
3. See 2 Samuel 11:1-4 (AMP)
4. See Hebrews 10:25 (AMP
5. See Proverbs 26:14 (AMP)
6. See Exodus 20:17 (AMP)
7. See Psalm 51:3 (AMP)
8. See Proverbs 28:13 (AMP)
9. See Psalm 51:4 (AMP)
10. See 1 John 1:9 (AMP)
11. See Psalm 51:1 (AMP)
12. See Psalm 37:5 (AMP)
13. See 1 John 2:15-16 (AMP)
14. See James 4:4 (AMP)
15. See 1 John 5:4-5 (AMP)
16. See Ephesians 4:22-24 (AMP)

Chapter 7: After a Fall

1. See Proverbs 24:16 (AMP)
2. See Psalm 27:4 (AMP)
3. See Jude 24 (AMP)

Chapter 8: How to Escape

1. See 1 Corinthians 10:13 (AMP)
2. See Galatians 4:9 (AMP)
3. See Hebrews 12:1 (AMP)

Chapter 9: Reaching Your Potential

1. See Matthew 19:21-22 (AMP)
2. See Genesis 32:24-28 (AMP)
3. See 1 Peter 5:10 (AMP)
4. See Hebrews 6:1 (AMP)
5. See Romans 6:12 (AMP)
6. See 2 Corinthians 7:1 (AMP)
7. See Mark 6:56 (AMP)
8. See Psalm 119:67 (AMP)

Chapter 10: Accountability and Connectivity

1. See Proverbs 27:17 (AMP)
2. See 2 Corinthians 5:18 (AMP)
3. See Revelation 3:20 (AMP)
4. See Hebrews 10:25 (AMP)
5. See Genesis 2:18 (KJV)
6. See Psalm 19:7-9 (KJV)
7. See Psalm 50:5 (AMP)
8. See Proverbs 31:1l (AMP)

Chapter 11: Becoming His Son

1. See John 1:12 (AMP)
2. See Psalm 16:11 (AMP)
3. See Acts 9:6 (AMP)
4. See Matthew 25:40 (AMP)
5. See Matthew 25:15 (AMP)
6. See Luke 1:38 (AMP)
7. See Romans 14:12 (AMP)
8. See Colossians 3:23 (AMP)
9. See Luke 19:17 (KJV)
10. See Philippians 2:5-7 (AMP)

Chapter 12: Purity

1. See 2 Corinthians 7:1 (AMP)
2. See Romans 12:1 (AMP)
3. See 1 Peter 2:9, 10 (AMP)
4. See 1 John 1:9 (KJV)
5. See Romans 6:22 (AMP)

Chapter 13: Finding Your Place in His Presence

1. See Hebrews 4:16 (AMP)
2. See Exodus 19:10, 11 (AMP)
3. See Exodus 20:18-20 (AMP)
4. See Hebrews 10:19-23 (AMP)
5. See John 14:26 (AMP)
6. See Psalm 20:6 (AMP)
7. See Psalm 121:5 (AMP)
8. See Isaiah 10:27 (KJV)
9. See Acts 1:8 (AMP)
10. See Romans 6:1-18 (AMP)
11. See 1 Corinthians 6:17 (AMP)
12. See Galatians 2:20 (AMP)
13. See Exodus 33:17 (AMP)
14. See Psalm 96:9 (KJV)

15. See Psalm 42:2 (KJV)
16. Matthew 5:6 (KJV)
17. See Isaiah 59:2 (AMP)
18. See 1 John 1:10 (AMP)
19. See Romans 13:14 (AMP)
20. See 1 Corinthians 12:14 (AMP)

Chapter 14: A New Beginning

1. See 2 Corinthians 5:17 (AMP)
2. See Psalm 107:9 (AMP)
3. See Ephesians 4:22-23 (KJV)
4. See Philippians 3:13 (KJV)
5. See Romans 7:18 (KJV)
6. See John 8:36 (AMP)
7. See 1 Peter 4:1, 2 (KJV)
8. See Psalm 32:5 (AMP)
9. See Proverbs 28:13 (AMP)
10. See Ephesians 2:8-9 (KJV)
11. See James 4:7 (KJV)
12. See Isaiah 26:3 (KJV)
13. See Psalm 119:35 (KJV)
14. See Deuteronomy 8:6 (KJV)
15. See Colossians 3:2 (KJV)
16. See Proverbs 18:21 (KJV)
17. See Psalm 40:3 (KJV)
18. See Philippians 4:13 (KJV)
19. See Philippians 4:19 (AMP)
20. See 2 Timothy 1:7 (AMP)
21. See Psalm 27:1 (AMP)
22. See 1 John 4:4 (AMP)
23. See 2 Corinthians 2:14 (AMP)
24. See 1 Corinthians 1:30 (KJV)
25. See 1 Peter 2:24 (KJV)
26. See 1 Peter 5:7 (KJV)
26. See 2 Corinthians 3:17 (KJV)

Chapter 15: Healing Your Marriage

[1.]   See Luke 4:23 (AMP)
[2.]   See Matthew 16:24 (KJV)
[3.]   See Philemon 1:6 (KJV)
[4.]   See Ephesians 4:29 (AMP)
[5.]   See Matthew 12:36 (KJV)
[6.]   See Genesis 2:18 (KJV)
[7.]   See Luke 17:3 (KJV)
[8.]   See Mark 11:23-26 (KJV)
[9.]   See 1 Peter 3:8-12 (KJV)
[10.]   See John 3:16 (KJV)
[11.]   See Luke 6:38 (KJV)

CPSIA information can be obtained at www.ICGtesting.com
Printed in the USA
LVOW082241160613

338825LV00001B/35/P